# PLYO-FLEX

## Plyometrics and Flexibility Training for Explosive Martial Arts Kicks and Performance Sports

### Jump higher, run faster, be stronger, kick better!

By

**Marc De Bremaeker**

*Fons Sapientiae Publishing*

**PLYO-FLEX - Plyometrics and Flexibility Training for Explosive Martial Arts Kicks and Performance Sports**. 3 rd Edition published in 2018 by Fons Sapientiae Publishing, Cambridge, United Kingdom. The First Edition of this work was published in 2013.

ISBN for the printed version, 3rd edition: 978-0-9957952-6-6

### *Recommended reading, by the same author*:

"Advanced Krav Maga: A Complete Reference" (2018)
"Joint Kicks - Destruction of the Opponent's Limbs" (2018)
"Isoplex - Musculation Program for an Aesthetic and Truly Athletic Body" (2017)
"Krav Maga Kicks - Kicking for No-nonsense Self-preservation" (2017)
"Sacrifice Kicks - Flying, Hopping, Jumping and Suicide Kicks" (2016)
"Stealth Kicks - The Forgotten Art of Ghost Kicking" (2015)
"Ground Kicks-Advanced Martial Arts Kicks for Goundfighting" (2015)
"Stop Kicks-Jamming, Obstructing, Stopping, Impaling, Cutting and Preemptive Kicks" (2014)
"Low kicks-Advanced Martial Arts Kicks for Attacking the Lower Gates" (2013)
"Plyo-Flex-Plyometrics and Flexibility Training for Explosive Martial Arts Kicks" (2013)
"The Essential Book of Martial Arts Kicks" (2010) by Tuttle Publishing
"Le Grand Livre des Coups de Pied" (2018) by Budo Edition (in French)
"i Calci nelle Arti Marziali" (2015) by Edizioni Mediterranee (in Italian)
"Les Coups de Pied d'Arret" (2017) (in French)
"Les Coups de Pied Bas" (2016) (in French)
"Les Coups de Pied au Sol" (2018) (in French)

# DEDICATION

This book is dedicated to my wife and life companion of over forty years. Without her love and support, nothing would have seen the light of day. Being an athlete in her own right, she knows about hard work and long hours.

**Aviva Giveoni**

Dear Reader,

In this day and age, the life of a serious author has become quite difficult. The proliferation of books and the explosion of internet content has made it nearly impossible to promote work based on extensive research and requiring complex lay-out. Please enjoy this book. Once you are finished, I would ask kindly that you take a few short minutes to give your honest opinion. A unbiased Amazon review, of even a few words only, would be highly appreciated and encouraging.

Thank You,

*Marc*

**To practice five things under all circumstances constitutes perfect virtue; these five are gravity, generosity of soul, sincerity, earnestness, and kindness.**
**~Confucius**

# ACKNOWLEDGEMENTS

Thank you to my co-author and technical adviser to this book, *Roy Faige*. For his un-wavering support in spite of all the difficulties we had on the way, for his life-long friendship and for hours of arduous training, he should be commended.

Late Sensei *Sidney Shlomo Faige* should be mentioned as the central pivot of my Martial Arts career.

*Sensei Sydney Faige in action*

Thank you to the dedicated Martial Artists who posed for the photographs and the drawings: *Roy Faige, Ziv Faige, Gil Faige, Dotan De Bremaeker, Nimrod de Bremaeker, Shay Levi, Tamir Carmi, Itay Leibovich ...*

*Roy and Marc*

Special thanks to *Shahar Navot*, the professional illustrator and Martial artist who did all the drawings for my previous book ("Essential Book of Martial Arts Kicks"). Shahar could not participate to this work, but he should be mentioned: Everything I know about illustrating, I learned from him. Our previous collaboration has taught me so much, but I am still very far from getting close to his talent.

Some of the photographs have been extracted from previous photos sessions book by gifted professional photographer *Guli*

*Dotan De Bremaeker*

*Cohen.* Other photographs have been taken by my life partner *Aviva Giveoni* and by talented *Grace Wong*.

## Success is no accident. It is hard work, perseverance, learning, studying, sacrifice and most of all, love of what you are doing or learning to do.
## ~Pele

# CONTENTS

Afterword

# Foreword to the "Kicks" Series

## A goal is not always meant to be reached, it often serves simply as something to aim at.
## ~Bruce Lee

*The 'Foreword' is very similar to those of the previous book in the 'Kicks' series. In order to spare a near re-read to our faithful readers of 'Low Kicks', 'Stop Kicks', 'Ground Kicks', 'Stealth Kicks', 'Sacrifice Kicks','Krav Maga Kicks' and 'Joint Kicks' we invite you to go directly to the* Introduction *on page 20.*

My Martial Arts career started with Judo at age 6. Judo was pretty new Fifty years ago, and a bit mystical in the Western World. A mysterious Oriental Art teaching how to use one's opponent's strength against him was a pretty attractive proposition for a wimpy kid. And the decorum and costume trappings made it a unique selling proposition. That is, until the Kung Fu craze of the Seventies, starring Bruce Lee, and then others.

In my opinion, what fascinated the Western masses, and the teen-ager I was then, was mostly the fantastic kicking maneuvers in the spectacular fights of those Kung-Fu movies. The bulk of the fight scenes were based on spectacular exchanges, the likes of which we had never seen before. What was new and revolutionary back then, may seem banal and common to today's younger reader. But we had been raised in the era of boxing and we had been conditioned by the fair-play of *Queensburry's* rules: we had no idea one could fight *like that*!

It was also the first time that the general public in Europe and America had seen a well-rounded Martial Art in action: punching, but also striking, kicking, throwing down, grappling, locking... It comprised all fighting disciplines in seamless aggregation. Wow! Judo was great, but I now wanted to *kick* like Bruce Lee. I therefore took up *Shotokan Karate*. 'Shotokan-ryu' is not the most impressive kicking style, but it was then the most developed Kicking Art outside of Asia and the only one available to me. It is as well and I certainly do not regret it. Though it is not an art known for extravagant kicks, Shotokan is very well organized didactically. It also emphasizes tradition, hard training, focus (*Zanshin*) and mastery of basic work. In all athletic endeavors, the continuous drilling of basic work at all levels of proficiency is the only real secret to success. Shotokan Karate drills and low training stances definitely fit this bill.

So, during the whole of my career, I kept practicing Shotokan Karate, or a Shotokan-derived style at all times. I also kept at Judo, my first love. But in parallel, I started to explore other Arts a few years at the time, as opportunities and geography allowed. During my long Martial Arts career, I also did practice assiduously Karatedo from the *Kyokushinkai, Shotokai, Wadoryu* and *Sankukai* schools. I also trained for long stints of *TaeKwonDo, Muay Thai, Krav Maga, Capoeira, Savate-Boxe Française*, two styles of traditional *Ju-Jitsu* and some soft styles o*f Kung Fu*. This search is where I developed my individual methods and my own understanding of the Art of Kicking and its place in complex fighting. It also provided the basis on which to build my own personal research. Of course, this is strongly accented towards the type of maneuvers and training that favor my personal physiology and personality, but I have tried very hard to keep an open mind, among others through coaching.

Sometimes during this maybe too eclectic career, my travels took me to the **Shi-Heun**

School of the late *Sensei Sidney Faige*, mentioned in the Acknowledgements. The *Shi-Heun* style is *Shotokan*-derived and mixed with *Judo* practice. It emphasizes extreme conditioning, total fighting under several realistic rules sets and the personal quest for what works best for oneself. And its self-defense training is based on no-nonsense *Krav Maga.* As this was only the early Eighties, this was definitely a prophetic ancestor of today's phenomena of Mixed Martial Arts of 'UFC' fame. The free-fighting rules in the *Dojo* were 'all-out' and 'to-the-ground', but this did not hinder the success of the School's students in more traditional tournaments under milder rules. The direct disciples of *Sensei Faige* did indeed roam the tournament scene undefeated for years.

*Sensei Sidney Faige*

In these days, points tournament fighting was mainly WUKO (World Union of Karate Organizations), with some notable exceptions like *Kyokushinkai* and *Semi-contact Karate* bouts. Unfortunately, WUKO generally (boringly) consisted in two competitors safely jumping up-and-down and waiting for the other to initiate a move, in order to stop-reverse-punch him to the body.

When my name was called up in these events, there was usually some spontaneous applause from the spectators; they knew they were going to see, finally, some kicking. I apologize if it sounds like boasting; the point I am trying to make is that Karate fans of these times came to see kicking and rich fighting moves, and not some unrealistic form of boxing. And this is not to denigrate *Karatedo*, but more the castrating effect of unintelligent rules sets.

*Sensei Faige with the winning Israeli National Team; the author and Roy Faige are on the right*

*Marc and Roy facing off at the finals of a 1987 Points Tournament*

*Marc, kicking in point tournament*

It is my strong belief that Kicking is what made the Oriental Martial arts so appealing. As I have already mentioned in articles and previous books, I do firmly argue that *kicking is more effective than punching.* This usually causes many to stand up, disagree and maybe want to *punch* me. This is an old debate, still raging, and I respectfully ask to be allowed to complete the sentence. I strongly believe that kicking is more effective than punching, *but proficiency takes much more time and work.* When presented this way, I do hope that this opinion is more acceptable to most. Let me detail my position briefly.

### Kicking is more efficient than punching:

1. Because of the longer range

2. Because the muscles of the leg are much bigger and powerful than those of the arms

3. Because kicking targets, unlike punching targets, go from head all the way down to toes

4. Because kicks are less expected and therefore more surprising than punches, especially at shorter ranges

I readily admit that the opponents of my position do have valid arguments. They will point out that kicks are inherently slower than punches and can be easily jammed be-

*One needs to drill kicks from very close ranges as well*

cause they start from longer ranges. They will also point out that kicking often opens the groin, while forgetting that so does punching usually as well. It is my experience that, - *after a lot of dedicated and intelligent work-,* many kicks can be *as swift as punches and can be delivered at all ranges and from all positions.*

During all my training years, I invested a lot of time, personal drilling and original research into Kicking Arts from all over the world. I experimented with all training tips gathered and I endeavored to try all mastered new kick variations in actual free-fighting and competitive tournaments. Here is the place to note that this is *not* about a huge number of different techniques; it is about finding the best possible techniques suited to one's specific strength, physiology and affinities (Once you have found your few techniques and the best way to drill them, then you focus on fast and perfect execution from all ranges and positions). During my quest in the realm of kicking, I slowly developed a personal kicking style based on my personal history and mindset. I researched most of the available literature, but very few treatises were actually *dedicated* to kicking. The few works I found about kicking were generally very good, but usually style-restricted and unorganized. I never found the kind of book that I would have liked to have at the start of my Martial arts career. And so I decided to write it myself and share my global view of the subject. To the best of my knowledge, there has never been an attempt to compile and organize all the different Kick types and variation in such a way that it could serve as a reference work and the basis for exploration for the kick-lover. I did try to start this potentially huge work, probably imperfectly, with a series of Books I chose to name the 'Kicks series'. A global overview of Basic Kicks was presented in **'The Essential Book of Martial Arts Kicks'** (Tuttle). Its success lead me to follow with the important lower gates attacks in **'Low Kicks'**, and then **'Stop Kicks'** about preempting, jamming, impaling, obstructing and 'cutting' Kicks. As a sign of these MMA times, the series was naturally enriched by **'Ground Kicks'**. We continued this work with this, **'Stealth Kicks'**, covering misdirection and dissimulation while kicking; and went on to cover airborne and suicide-kicking with **'Sacrifice Kicks'**. No-nonsense practical kicking for Self-defense was covered in **'Krav Maga Kicks'**, and **'Joint Kicks'**. We hope that all this work will be built upon by others in the future. As mentioned and underlined many times, kicking proficiency requires a lot of serious drilling. I have therefore also published this work about the basic general drills that will help you reach higher levels of proficiency. As in all athletic endeavors, it is the basic drills that will build the strong foundation needed; and it is to those basic drills that the truly good athlete will come back for further progress again and again. **'Plyo-Flex Training for Explosive Martial Arts Kicks and Other Performance Sports'** does present those general, basic but so-important exercises that one should regularly practice for continuous improvement of kicking proficiency. Get to work then!

And now last, but certainly not least: it is important to underline that my strong views do not try in any way or form to denigrate the Punching Arts. My personal philosophy is that Martial arts are a whole with a world of possible emphasis. A complete Martial artist should be proficient in punching, kicking, moving, throwing, grappling, evading and more. An experienced Artist will have his own preferences and particular skills in his own way to look at the Martial Arts as a whole. And here must I add the obvious: *there is no kicking mastery* without punching proficiency! Even for a dedicated kicker, punching will be needed for closing the gap, feinting, setting up a kick, following it up and much more... This will be made abundantly clear from most of the applications presented in this volume, just as it is clear from all my previous work.

It must be said that Punching is sometimes the best or the only answer in some situations. I have known and met some extraordinary Punching Artists using kicks only as feints or set-ups. On the other hand, great kickers like legendary *Bill 'Superfoot' Wallace* were extremely skilled punchers and working hard at it, as I personally experienced in a few seminars. Kick and Punch, Punch and Kick: well-rounded is the secret.

And this leads me naturally to my last point. I would not want my books and my views to be misunderstood as an appeal to always kick when fighting, and especially not as an appeal to always high-kick. The best kicker in the world should not execute a high Kick, *just because he can*. A Kick should only be delivered *because and when it is suitable* to a specific situation! Obvious maybe, but certainly worth reminding. In someone else's words:

## Take things as they are. Punch when you have to punch. Kick when you have to kick.
## ~Bruce Lee

# Introduction

Fighting is a well-rounded physical activity: It requires strength, speed, endurance, agility, explosiveness, flexibility, core musculature and mental qualities. No wonder it was at the core of the ancient original Olympic Games.

Today's fighter, besides his particular technical training, usually runs short and long distances, skips rope, trains with weights and weight machines, and does complementary cross training activities.

This book is focused on the kicking skills of Martial Arts of all types, but it is highly relevant to all athletic activities requiring power, flexibility and explosiveness. The drills presented are simple and versatile; they generally are not Martial Arts-specific. The more specific kicking drills are variations of basic drills designed to arouse more interest with the fighter; they can be executed easily by athletes from other fields if they so wish, but they can also be disregarded with no impact on the overall system success.

It has been the premise of my previous book that kicking is a superior skill to punching but requires much more training. Fans of the MMA fights like the UFC have surely noticed that knock-outs by punches come usually at the end of a series of punches; but the much rarer knock-out by kicks comes after a single well-timed technique. Whether one agrees or not, one will have to concur that effective kicking requires especially hard training. Besides the regular technical training in one's chosen discipline, a few specific kicking training exercises have

*Example of one of many kicking drills*

been presented in the previous volume mentioned. Those were just simple drills specific to the given technique and only given as examples. It is clear that the amount and variety of possible exercises to improve kicking skills are huge. Some more will be presented at the end of this book.

*Another example of Kicking Drill*

Every school and training camp has its own kicking routines and drill sets to both improve the kicking techniques of the students and their general physical stamina and preparedness. Those classic training drills are well known and used, and most of them will be categorized at the end of this book, just as a reference and invitation to the reader to further research them. The well-prepared kicker will train his muscles for strength, his techniques for speed and accuracy, his free-fighting for timing and positioning, his heart and lungs for stamina, and more; just like any other athlete.

But, in the opinion of the author, there are two categories of exercise that are under-used for many reasons and that really can bring kicking mastery to a superior level: *Plyometrics* and *Flexiometrics*. The **methodical** drilling of those two categories of exercises, in tandem, do bring exceptional progress. And this is not only true for Martial arts and Martial arts kicks: *all sportsmen can benefit from the drills presented*, in spite of the fact that they are sometimes a bit specific. By doing these drills in an organized fashion, one will run faster, jump higher, develop more power and perform better, **in any activity**. But as two sides of the same coin, Plyometrics and Flexibility Training, ***must be drilled simultaneously and methodically.***

***Plyometrics*** could be defined as *the drilling for explosiveness*. **Explosiveness** could be defined in turn, for sports, as *a combination of power and speed*. This definition makes immediately very clear how important it is for the "kicking" part of the art. The principle behind this kind of exercise is that you drill the muscle by contracting it eccentrically and then immediately, concentrically. The theory and physiology behind it is not of great importance for our purpose, but will be hinted at in the relevant chapter. Just remember that you will usually stretch the muscle before shocking it into contracting. For anybody doubting the bump in performance he can expect from serious plyometrics training, the generally agreed upon history of its development would be of interest. The Russians dominated track and field athletics in the Fifties, until the secret of their success was discovered as the training techniques of Coach *Yuri Verkhoshansky*. Only once these techniques became generally used and refined all over the world, did the field level. *Plyometrics* started to be used in all sports with great success. There are today many variations and denominations, like "Kinetic energy accumulation training" or "Shock training", but the basic ideas behind the drills are the same. Some of the exercises presented will even be outside the physiological theory presented, as what is important for us is not the pure sport science, but the contribution of the drill to more explosive kicking or athletic performance.

It is the author's opinion that *Plyometrics* are not used enough in Martial Arts for two basic reasons. **One**: *Plyometrics* have sometimes the bad reputation of being dangerous and detrimental to the joints. To this we reply that *Plyometrics* are a tool and it is the way it is used that will make it beneficial or detrimental. Cautious and gradual drilling will ensure no harm is done while huge progress is achieved.

**The other reason** is probably because it does not look much like Martial Arts and is therefore not sexy enough for class practice where students expect high kicks and a lot of fighting action. Jumping off boxes does not come close to the enjoyment of free fighting... This is why we have tried in this book to present as many as possible drills including kicking, whether pure plyometric or hybrid.

**Flexiometrics** is an invented word in the spirit of *Plyometrics*. It should mean something like **Intensive Stretching**. The exercises are not new or based on any novel theory. The word comes in here to try to underline the fact that a lot of investment in Stretching is required for explosive kicking, much more than what is usually done. Much too often, stretching is part of the warm-up and cool-down of training sessions, and that's it. Although it is extremely important to stretch before and after training, this should not be considered Flexibility Training. The serious Martial Arts Kicker should have dedicated stretching training sessions at least three times a week, session not shorter than one hour. This is the second "secret" of explosive kicking, and it should be noted that it is not limited to success in high kicking: it will give the same performance boost to medium and low kicking. "*Flexiometrics*" is therefore, for us, the systematic and separate work on stretching and flexibility that will benefit the kicker. A minimal amount of theory about flexibility will be presented in the relevant chapter, but it is the

Yoga-type work that is favored by the author. In fact, the Martial Artist who has the time and opportunity should cross-train with Yoga for optimal results. If time is not available, let him concentrate on the exercises presented here.

*Flexibility training is key for the success of the Kicking Artist*

Again, the author feels that Flexibility Training is looked down upon because it takes away precious time from sexier martial art training, and also because most artists do not understand its importance. Flexible artists tend to believe they do not need it, and stiff ones are happy with their techniques and do believe that the time needed for some small eventual improvement is justified. They are both wrong. It is true that flexibility improvements require time and methodical training but they will bring, much faster than thought, huge progress to kicking speed and range.

Many feel that flexibility is a genetic given and that not much can be done if one is born stiff. It is true that genetics are important, and that one should start exercising his flexibility as early as possible. But one's flexibility can greatly be improved by regular and intensive training. It has been shown by academic research, and time and again proven in practice with our students; there is no doubt about it.

It should be noted that this book does not pretend to be exhaustive. It will present a range of exercises that the author feels should be practiced by the Martial Art kicking artist. But there are many more possible drills, probably all beneficial. There would be no point in an encyclopedic presentation of the subject, and the reader is invited to do his own research and devise his own variations.

Of course, *Plyometrics* and *Flexiometrics* are not enough to make you a master kicker. But all other training exercises being equal, the author feels that they are the two secret ingredients that will bring your kicking abilities to the next level. The reader is invited to do alternating sessions of Plyometrics and Flexiometrics based on the drills presented, and see for himself after only a few weeks. The preferred schedule would be:

Monday: *Flex*

Tuesday: *Plyo*

Wednesday: *Flex*

Thursday: *Plyo*

Friday: *Flex*

Saturday and Sunday: None of the above.

One full day rest a week without any type of training at all is highly

*Flexibility training should start as early as possible, but can be greatly improved at any age*

recommended. It must be underlined, and will be explained later, that training routines should be fixed, for at least a month: Changing exercises on account of not getting bored is not conducive to optimal progress. Routines should be changed after three months regular continuous use.

# PART 1

# PLYOMETRICS

**A dream doesn't become reality through magic; it takes sweat, determination and hard work.**
**~Colin Powell**

# CHAPTER 1  GENERAL

## 1.1   Principles

The Merriam-Webster dictionary defines plyometrics as: *"exercise involving repeated rapid stretching and contracting of muscles (as by jumping and rebounding) to increase muscle power"*. The stretching before contracting ensures a more intense contraction, and therefore more explosive power. The use of "explosive" tries to convey a dimension of time to the qualities gained by such training: The muscles trained will so be stronger *while contracting faster at peak power*.

*Muscle strength* is the maximum force one can squeeze out of his muscles, like the heaviest weight one can lift. *Muscle power* is: achieving this full strength <u>*fast*</u>.
A muscle needs to contract in order to cause movement. It has been demonstrated that this *concentric* contraction will be all the more energetic if the muscle has been stretched immediately before in what is called *eccentric* contraction, storing in fact some elastic energy. In layman's terms, you get more bang for the buck if you lengthen your muscle just before you contract it into the required move, and this because it adds the energy from your muscle elasticity to the whole equation. This is often referred to as the *stretch shortening cycle*. A muscle stretched just before it contracts will do so with more energy. As the muscles become used to the extra power, they become more efficient at storing elastic energy. The total amount of power exerted during the exercise is more than with regular exercise, therefore causing more muscle potential power with time. The muscles become able to go from the eccentric contraction to the concentric contraction faster, thus creating "peak power" – fast maximum energy. This is what is referred to as "shortening the stretch cycle".
This is one of the reasons why most exercises should be executed in a "multi-response" way, meaning in series and **with no pause in between the jumps**. *Multi-response* keeps fast alternating of stretch and contract, and challenges the muscle accordingly. All exercises should be started single-response to let the body familiarize itself with the specific move. Then, when adequate, one should gradually strive to go multi-response: back and forth fast and with no rest.

There is much more to the full physiological theory than what has been presented: there is a part played by the *myotatic reflex*, which is the automatic contraction of a stretched muscle; and a neurological part played by same "stretch" reflex which lowers the body's tendency to automatically limit maximum power exerted. Plyometrics drills will therefore improve gradually the neuro-muscular interactions while allowing for the highest possible energy application in training. The several existing theories on how and why it works are probably all valid and complement each other.

For the reader who is interested in the theories behind *Plyometrics* and wants to dwell into the very interesting physiological details, I would recommend the works of the "father" of modern Plyometrics: *Prof. Yuri Verkhoshansky*. His works are readily available in English and extremely detailed.

## 1.2   Caution

*Plyometrics* are not for the untrained. Some coaches have given them a bad reputation and are firmly against their practice on the grounds of safety. They argue that the benefits are largely outweighed by the damage they can cause, because they apply to the muscles, joints and connective tissues more energy than what they are built for. The author will argue that it is exactly what sport is about: furthering gradually the border of human potential, with the emphasis on **gradually**. All physical activities lead to some fiber destruction that will allow the body to re-build stronger fibers to adapt to what is regularly asked from the same body. Ask, -slowly-, more and more of your body and it will adapt. Accordingly, only *Plyometrics* will be able to let you access the next stage of muscular explosive power.

*Plyometrics* have, in fact, a proven long-term effect of injury prevention; but it should be underscored that these exercises have to be taken up very gradually and after a minimum level of muscle tone has been achieved. Because all their purpose is to maximize the amount of energy applied to the muscles, tendons and joints, it is easy to understand that they require slow and methodical implementation.

The assiduous martial artist will have no problems doing them, but still should increase the length of a dedicated plyometrics session gradually *from 5 minutes on*. He should also ensure that he is properly warmed up, and stop at the first sign of joint pain.

The beginner will have to develop regular muscle strength first by regular training and muscle-building exercises. Only after a few months, should he start carefully doing these drills, after warm-up, and under professional supervision.

A plyometric session should start with a ten minutes warm-up and light stretching. Then **five minutes** of plyometric exercises. *No more*. Then five minutes cool-down stretching. The "plyometrics" part of the session can then be increased by a weekly five more minutes, with caution and stopping at the first hint of joint pain. The cool down should become a full ten minutes. Altogether, a training session *should never go over one hour*, which means about **forty net minutes of high energy plyos**.

Training sessions should be two a week at the start, then three a week, *but never more*.

Plyometrics should not be done day after day, and there always should be *one day in between sessions*.

It is recommended to practice on *soft flooring*, like grass or indoor sports halls. Never on hard floors like concrete. The wearing of running trainers, reducing impact shock, can be of big help.

Above all, the practicing artist is advised to use common sense and to listen to his body.

## 1.3    *Martial Arts and Plyometrics*

From the Introduction and all the above, it should now be clear to the reader why *Plyometrics* are so important to the Martial Artist, and especially to the kicker: **delivery of the maximum energy faster!**
Not only will *Plyometrics* increase the power of each kick, it will also allow for faster movement of body positioning, all the while contributing to the overall fitness and endurance. Some of the drills have also a direct contribution to some kicks and moves. Flying Kicks are obvious, but also Hopping kKcks, hip thrusts in Penetrating Kicks and much more.
The martial artist should include dedicated Plyometrics training sessions in his routine; noticeable results will come quickly. He should do so in parallel with serious Flexibility training.
Here is the place to stress an important point: Do train per fixed routines **for at least one month but no more than three**. The body needs time to rebuild itself as per the stimuli you are going to impose on it, and each drill works in its own specific way.

In this day and age of instant gratification and minimal attention span, people tend to want too much variation to avoid "boredom". Varying exercises from session to session *is not conducive to optimum progress*. For at least a month, **but preferably three**, you should drill the same exercises and force your body to make progress on them, working faster or jumping higher gradually. On the other hand, after three months, when you have made good progress, your body has become accustomed to the drills and the progress will become incrementally smaller and slower. Then, *and only then*, is the time to trick your body in having to make new efforts and adapt itself to new drills. This is an important rule; the author has seen too many promising fighters squandering their training time in sexy and ever-changing training sessions. ***Slow, steady and methodical takes the race!***

Regarding the training sessions, the author is not a proponent of giving out lists of exercises as a training session. This work is aiming at experienced artists and athletes who will know how to organize their sessions and which exercises to choose from all those presented in the book. A plyometric training session should be dedicated to *Plyometrics* only and should not be over an hour. The drilling must be as intense as possible, with as little rest as possible between the drills, but of course, that is highly dependent on the stamina and level of fitness of the trainee. With progress, the artist will be able to cram more exercises gradually. Do not over-train though; *longer than one hour sessions would be counter-productive.*

## 1.4    *The Golden Rules of Plyometrics Training*

These rules are extremely important, both for your safety and for optimal progress. Write them down and keep them always in mind, or written on the wall.
See next page:

**1.4.1 ALWAYS warm-up and stretch before practice** (Dynamic stretching for overall muscle heating and lengthening).

**1.4.2 Start slowly and increase intensity gradually,** both within the session and from session to session.

**1.4.3 ALWAYS stretch after a session** (Static stretching for flexibility maintenance).

**1.4.4 Train with intent and minimize ground contact time.** Concentrate on explosiveness, both physically and mentally.

**1.4.5 Do not over-train.** It would be detrimental to your progress. Time must be given to the muscles to rebuild themselves in the improved configuration. And remember that other aspects of training need attention. Two sessions a week is optimal, and, in any case, NEVER more than three.

**1.4.6 Build strength in parallel** with regular weight training drills. Remember that strength is a part of the explosiveness equation.

**1.4.7 Drill fixed routines.** Do the same exercises weekly and do not try to change and innovate all the time. Change routines after three months.

# CHAPTER 2  GROUND DRILLS

*Those are the exercises that can be done without any special equipment. The drills are simple jumps, from and back to the ground. Please note that even the drills looking like kicking maneuvers should be practiced by non-martial arts athletes. They are important, not only because they are effective, but also because they can be executed any time, any place.* **Do not practice on hard concrete floors though!**

## 2.1 *Flying Butt Kick*

From a standing position, slightly bend the knees and straighten down the arms. Jump up *as high as possible* while trying to kick your own butt with your heels. Try to keep your arms down and straight. Land while bending the knees. Once you are familiar with the move, do it **in series**, so that you jump up immediately from the bent-knees landing position.

*Jump high without taking up momentum downwards and kick yourself in the butt*

*Flying Butt kick*

### Key points:
• *Keep your arms down* in order to avoid their "helping" your jump.
• *Explode up* with intent and really try to kick yourself.
• In series, *minimize ground time.*

This will remind the trainee of another kicking drill for the high chambering of the Front Kick in which one **heel-kicks his own backside before delivering the penetrating front kick**. See Photos at the top of next page.

➡

*Kick your backside on your way to the regular Front Kick chamber: a great technical drill*

## 2.2 Flying Double Knee Kick

From a standing position, bend the knees and place your arms parallel to the floor as a target for the knee kicks. Explode up **as high as possible** and try to knee the palms. Try not to move the arms as a "help" to your jump, consider them immovable targets. Once you are familiar with the move, start to work **in series** with no pauses in between.

*Try to envision the drill as a real double flying knee strike*

### Key points:
- *Do not move the arms.*
- *Try to knee as high as possible.*
- *Minimize ground time.*

*Flying Knee Strike*

*Flying Double Knee drill*

In a variation of this drill in series, you can also *progress gradually forward* from jump to jump. This is certainly a great drill for proficiency in Flying Knee Kicks.

## 2.3 Flying Double Wide Knee Kick

This is a variation of the previous drill. In this version, you simply jump with a **wide** Double Knee Kick **outside of your arms.** You bend the torso between the arms and knees. Once you have mastered the move, do it **in series** but with a pause in between the jumps. Once you feel ready, start working plyometrically **with minimum ground time** between the jumps.

*Wide Double Knee Flying Kick*

### Key Points:
- *Minimize ground time*.
- Make sure you *do not flex the legs* more than in photo 2.3.3; resist the temptation to start the jump from a crouching position.
- In this drill, concentrate on *lifting the knees as high as possible* outside the arms.

*A great drill for improved flying kicks*

## 2.4 Flying Front Kick

This drill is a hybrid of the first two drills, with a Karate twist. You jump off your two feet for a Flying Front Kick, making sure that the heel of the non-kicking leg hits your butt. As you land, you repeat the Kick with the same leg. See Photos at the top of next page.

### Key points:
- Kick off *from both feet*.
- When working in series, make sure *you kick from the same leg each time*, for the plyometric effect. Afterwards, do a full series with the other leg.
- *Kick high* and concentrate on the kick.
- Of course, *minimize ground time*.

*Flying Front Kicks in place, in series. Heel to butt*

## 2.5 Flying Twist

This is a variation of the Flying Double Knee Kick, important for regular- and Spinning-Flying Kicks. The principles are the same but you add a **twist** during the jump and land 180 degrees from starting position. This is a great drill, but **make sure you minimize ground time**.

This is an important drill for better spinning kicks.

*Flying Double Knee Kick with an airborne twist*

### Key points:
- Make sure you jump off *both feet simultaneously.*
- Concentrate on *lifting the knees high* and minimizing ground time.

*A great drill for better Spinning Kicks*

## 2.6 One-leg Fighting Stance Jump

Take a fighting stance on one knee, with the front leg bent at 90 degrees. Jump up **as high as possible**, pushing from both feet. Land in fighting stance, without knee/floor contact to avoid knee injury. Once you are familiar with the drill, repeat as fast as possible on one side. **The series are always one-sided only**. Afterwards, change sides and repeat.

*Jump up from one-kneed position*

### Key points:

- Avoid at any cost *landing on the knee*, directly in start position (at the cost of serious injury).
- Try to keep a *'fighting stance'* all the way.
- Concentrate on the *explosion up* from the one-kneed position.

This starting position also makes for a great regular kicking drill; see Photos.

*Front Kick from the one-knee position: a great drill*

These are all very similar to other well-known "ground" kicking drills from kneeling or one-kneed positions. Highly recommended and illustrated at the top of next page.

*Ground Front Kick from kneeling position*

*Ground Front Kick from One-Kneed Guard*

## 2.7 Lateral long jump

This is a very important exercise for speed of positioning.
Squat until you touch the ground with the tips of your fingers and *explode into the longest possible lateral jump*. Push off the outside leg while extending the inside leg. Stay low as you are trying to jump the **longest** possible distance, and not the highest jump. It is recommended to mark distance to strive for on the floor with 2 lines; with your progress, you will be able to gradually increase the distance between them. This drill needs to be practiced for length of jump first, before going to the multi response version (work in series).

Push off one foot for longest possible side jump

**Key points:**

- *Touch floor* and explode.
- Concentrate on *distance*, not height
- Work *in series* back and forth, touching floor each time, but with no pause.

The more advanced "Karate" version of the drill will be to add a *Side Kick* at the end of the side jump; each time! This is a very beneficial but challenging variation which I recommend warmly. Proceed gradually though.

*Lateral long jump capped with a side kick. Alternate sides with no pause*

*Touch floor before developing the side kick. Concentrate on good technique*

*When executing the drill, think about this kick*

One can see the similarity of execution with the extremely efficient "**Hand-on-floor Side Kick**" and is invited to refer to *The Essential Book of Martial Arts Kicks*.

## 2.8 Joined Legs Lateral Jump

In this drill, the focus must be on **speed** and *not* on height or distance. This is a typical multi-response drill, much used in many sport disciplines. It is recommended to use a marking on the floor or use a prop as a line to be jumped over back and forth.

From one side of the line, you jump laterally with your legs together. As you land on the other side, you jump off *immediately* back. And so forth.

There are two ways to practice this drill, and you should do both alternatively. In the first version, you jump back and forth in place. In the second version, necessitating a longer line on the floor, you jump both sideways and a bit forward, so progressing gradually forwards.

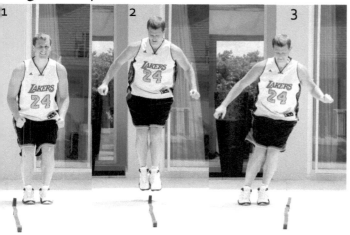

*Jump explosively back and forth over the line. This is the version with gradual forward progression*

### Key points:
- This is a *multi-response drill*: Concentrate on speed and explosiveness; minimize ground time.
- Do *not* try to jump high
- Do *both versions:* in place and going forwards

## 2.9 Hop into jumps

According to the plyometric theory, this is a purer way to execute the jumps already described before, and therefore **a more productive exercise** in terms of results. You simply do a small hop *just before* the higher jump and enjoy the fruits of the eccentric/concentric contraction couple. This method is highly recommended once you have mastered the jumps as described before. This execution requires more coordination, as you will have to remember to always hop before the jump, even when you work in series. So it will be: hop/jump/hop/jump/...

We shall illustrate the technique for the Flying Butt Kick (2.1) but it is valid for all other jumps, like the Flying Double Knee Kick, Flying Wide Double Knee Kick or Flying Front Kick.

The execution is pretty simple: *hop and immediately execute the Flying Butt Kick*. As you land, *immediately hop forward for another jump.*

Small hop, big jump. Minimize ground time

### Key points:
- This is pure plyometrics. Work *fast* with no pause at all.
- Explode *when the hop lands*.
- You can *mark the floor* for a fixed (*and then becoming gradually longer*) hop.

The coming Photos show the hop into a *Double Flying Knee Kick.*

Hop then double flying knee kick

An interesting variation is the **Hop into a Flying Kick**. Presented here is hopping into a Flying Front Kick. The principles are the same and you should strive to work *in series*, multi-response.

*Small hop, then jump up in flying front kick. Repeat*

## 2.10 *One-leg Butt Kick*

This is a more challenging version of the Flying Double Butt Kick (2.1): The whole drill is executed on one leg! Although it is harder on the muscles, it still has to be done *as fast as possible* in true plyometric fashion. Do not start this drill before you have fully mastered and have had a long practice of the Flying Double Butt Kick.

Stand on one leg with the lifted knee in front. Jump off the other leg and use it to kick your own butt. Once you have mastered the exercise, do it *in series* with minimum ground time. This is a punishing version, very difficult, but extremely beneficial to your explosiveness.

*Stand on one leg and kick your own butt repeatedly as fast as possible*

### Key points:
- Drill single-response thoroughly *before working in series*.
- Jump *as high* as possible.
- *Minimize ground time*.
- When working in series (multi-response), *use the same leg.* Then do a series with the other leg.

*The challenging one-leg butt kick*

## 2.11 *One-leg Lateral Jump*

This is obviously the more challenging one-legged variation of the classic lateral jumps (*2.7 and 2.8*). Standing on one leg you jump laterally *in series*, as fast as possible, but while jumping each time *as high as possible*. If not, it would just be the lateral hopping exercise presented just after this. *The jump is on the side of the standing leg.* You can mark the floor as a focusing help. This is a very difficult exercise if done properly, progress gradually.

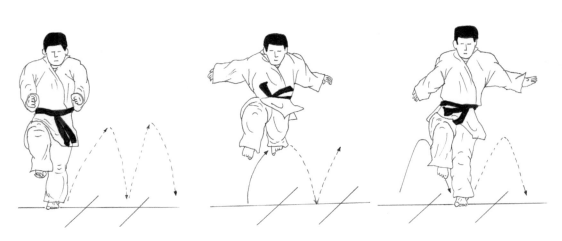

*On one leg, jump high and sideways. Repeat*

**Key points:**
- This is a difficult exercise; drill thoroughly *single response before going to series*.
- When working in series, do *concentrate on one leg*. Then drill the other leg in another series.
- The purpose of the exercise is *height*: concentrate on jumping high, then fast.

*A great drill to improve side kick positioning*

## 2.12 Lateral Hopping

This is the easier one-legged lateral drill, but still very important for explosive muscle

building. You just hop *back and forth* over a marked line on the floor. You can do this in place or going gradually forward. The key to this drill will *not* be height, but **speed**. There must be no pause whatsoever between the hops.

*Hop back and forth over line, as fast as possible*

## Key points:

- Concentrate on *minimizing ground time*. Work as fast as possible.
- Concentrate *on one leg until exhausted*; then switch to series with the other leg.

A kicking variation of this drill is presented in the next Figures. It is interesting to alternate between those two drill types for similar but synergistic results; and the kicking aspect gives it some more student interest. This will be a simple Hopping Side Kick series: hop sideways while kicking, and repeat. The purpose of the drill being the **lateral hop**, it is recommended to deliver low side kicks, in order to enable the trainee to concentrate o*n speed and hopping*, and not on the kicking. But once proficient, there is no reason why the trainee could not execute with higher kicks.

Stand on one leg, in typical Side Kick Chamber. Hop sideways while delivering the (low) side kick. Ideally, the jumping foot should touch the floor simultaneously with the full kick extension. Chamber back and repeat immediately.

*Lateral Hopping Low Side Kick in series*

## Key points:

- Concentrate on *speed* of hopping, not the kick.
- Repeat for a *minimum of 20 hops* before switching legs.
- This is a relatively low impact exercise: *Repeat,* switching sides until legs hurt. No pain, no gain!

*Hopping Side Kick*

*The kick is delivered during the airborne phase*

The simple lateral hopping, -multi-response in the same direction-, is by itself a great muscle-building drill. You need room for its execution, and a beach would provide you for it with the added benefit of the extra effort need in the sand. Just make sure that you practice the drill with **both** versions per direction of the jumps: jumping *in the direction of the lifted leg* and jumping *in the direction of the standing leg*!

*The simple basic one-legged side hop: jump in the direction of the standing leg*

*The simple basic one-legged side hop: jump in the direction of the lifted leg*

**Perseverance is the hard work you do after you get tired of doing the hard work you already did.**
**~Newt Gingrich**

### 2.13 Push-up to High Jumps

This is the old classic '**Burpee**', and like all classics, it is a great drill which importance has been proven by time. One could argue that the push-up does not do much for the kicker, but it does improve stamina and it forces the trainee to take the right starting position for the drill. All in all, this is a very well rounded drill, and a must-practice one. From a standing position, semi-squat and place your hands on the floor. Immediately throw your legs back to a "plank pose". Do a fast straight-back push up, before throwing back your feet between your hands. From this position, jump up *as high as possible* while stretching your hands up. Land in semi-squat and repeat. Of course, there is no pause in between the phases, and the execution is one smooth move from beginning to end.

*Classical push-up to high jump. A must for the serious artist*

### Key points:

- Concentrate on no-pause between the end of the push-up and the high jump! It is basically a *plyometric "hop and jump"*.
- Land *on slightly bent knees*.

When proficient, the Artist is encouraged to transform the throwing back of his feet into a *Double Drop Back Kick*. The drill could be executed in front of a heavy bag to be kicked as hard as possible. Remember though that *the heart of the drill is the jump up.*

*The very powerful Double Drop Back Kick*

## 2.14 Long Jumps

This is a very efficient and simple drill but it requires space to execute. You simply jump *as far as possible* with joined legs, *in series*. This is a **long** jump, not a high jump. It is important to concentrate on distance and *minimize the pause of ground time*. A series of long jumps requires obviously a free field long enough, as ten jumps would be the minimal series length. Do not execute on concrete floors!

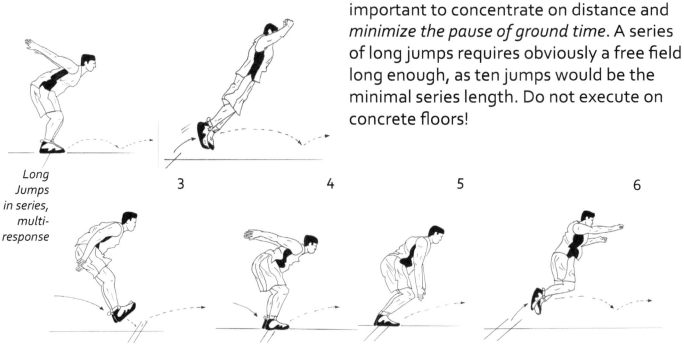

Long Jumps in series, multi-response

3          4          5          6

## Key points:

- As mentioned: *Length*, not height.
- Work *in series without rest*. The muscle-building effect comes from jumping off the "reception crouch" of the previous jump.
- *"Glue" legs together*.

Longest possible jump, legs together

Typical phases of the Long Jump Drill

Executing the Long Jump drill in sand makes it more challenging

*Even more challenging is to do the multi-response long jump in the sand and one-legged*

## 2.15 Flying Front Scissor Kicks in Series

This is an extremely beneficial drill that should be practiced by the Martial Artist at every session. Not only has it many explosiveness-building properties, but it is also a kicking drill in itself. The Kick practiced here is a versatile and very effective kick that should be kept in store by every kicking artist for the right opportunity (like in *Lyoto Machida's* UFC 129 fight against *Randy Couture*).

The drill is in fact simply the execution of the Double Flying Front Scissor Kick in series with no rest in between. This very important Kick, called *Nidan Geri* in Japanese *Karate*, is fast and difficult to block. It is a regular grounded rear-leg Penetrating Front Kick, immediately followed by a Flying Front Kick from the other leg; the switch between the kicking legs is done in a flying scissor way as the flying kick chamber starts as the regular kick recoil is still underway. There are many variations to the kick itself based on whether, among others, the first kick is a feint or a full kick, or whether the jump is high or long. But the principle stays the same, and so does the drill.

From a relatively high posture, do execute a full-power rear-leg Penetrating Front Kick. As you chamber the kick back, jump off your standing foot for a Flying Front Kick. The leg lifts in flying front kick chamber as the other leg is still recoiling from the regular grounded Front Kick. This causes an airborne scissor-move. After delivering the Flying

Front Kick, you chamber it back as you land on the first kicking foot. As soon as you land with the second kicking leg in front, you repeat the exercise; same side. Once you have mastered the drill, concentrate *on minimizing ground time during the series*. Try to do at least series of 10 kicks; then switch legs and execute the drill on the other side.

*Standing Kick, Scissor, ~ing Kick. In series, fast*

3      4      5      6

**Key points:**
- Master the technique first, *in single response*. Concentrate then on the kicking.
- Practice *in place first*; then, use a long free field to execute while kicking forward.
- Always remember that the plyometric purpose is to execute *in series without pause*.

### 2.16 Split Jumps

Here comes a classic which importance cannot be emphasized enough. This is a great explosive muscles-builder to be practiced regularly. **It must be noted that the drill must be executed after a good warm-up,** as there are some dangers of injury. In the same logic, it is a drill that must be approached *gradually* by the beginner or even the experienced artist that has abandoned it for some time.

You start in deep split guard position: the front leg is bent at 90 degrees and the back leg spread back and standing on the toes. The knee *does not* touch the floor and you face forward. Arms are locked in guard or *Hikite* position. Jump **up**, directly from the start position, *as high as possible* and switch the legs airborne. Land directly in the same starting position, but with opposite leg forward. *Repeat.*

*The classic sp[...] jumps*

**Key points:**
- *Warm up before the drill,* including stretching.
- Master the exercise *gradually and carefully*: Start single response and from a higher starting position.
- Once fully mastered, execute the exercise while concentrating on *minimal pause between the jumps.*

*Deep low front stance, jump up and switch sides*

*Make sure you start and finish in guard. In this version, reach up as you try to jump as high as possible*

This drill can be extended into an important "**Switch and Kick**" Drill that will be presented in section 4.6. The coming Photos illustrate the exercise.

*The full Split jump-and-front-kick-over-chair Drill. See section 4.6*

## 2.17 Frog Long Jumps

Here comes a great "frog walk" exercise that has long been a favorite of children Martial Arts classes. This is a fantastic plyometric drill if executed *in series and to its maximum*. As illustrated in the coming Figures, you start from the "frog" position: kneeling with your hands on the floors and elbows between the knees. You then jump as far as possible and reception yourself in the same frog position. This is a **long** jump, not high! Repeat immediately, with *minimal ground time*, until the muscles are exhausted.

*Playful but effective Frog Hops*

### Key Points:
- *Minimize ground time*.
- Jump *long* and close to the floor; do *not* try to jump high.
- Reception yourself *on the hands first,* before the feet land.

## 2.18 Abdominal Legs Throws

Now comes a classic *dojo* drill with partner. Unbeknownst to the trainees, it is a full plyometric drill, fantastic for the abdominals, the hip belt and the upper legs. Lying on your back, you catch your standing partner's ankles, as shown in the next illustrations. Using your abdominals, you lift your straight legs to 90 degrees. Your partner will forcefully throw your legs back towards the floor and you will brake the fall a few inches from the floor to lift the legs back up. Your partner will immediately throw the legs back down. Once you are familiar with the drill, your partner should use the maximum amount of force that will allow you to do the exercise and you shall strive to *minimize the amount of time at braking point* near the floor.

➡

*Your partner throws your legs
down, you lift them back a.s.a.p.*

### Key points:

- Legs *straight and together* at all times.
- *Back stays on the floor.*
- Stop *as close to the floor as possible* and lift back the legs *as soon as possible.*

There is a very well-known **variation** of the drill in which your partner throws your legs down *diagonally to your side* for extra- laterals work. You can do this variation by alternating sides or concentrating on one side before switching.

## 2.19 Pushed Lunges

Here comes a truly plyometric partner drill. It is again a lunge, but, this time, the extra energy for Plyometrics does not come from your jumping up but *from a partner pushing you.* As illustrated in the Figures at the top of next page, your partner pushes you forward and you land *as far as possible* in a lunge *as low as possible.* Your partner's push must be powerful but not jerky, and you must let yourself be pushed. The drill could stop at this stage with your going back fast and smoothly to start position for a repeat. But to make it more of a kicking drill and make full use of the plyometric aspect, you should come back to standing by executing a front-leg Front Kick directly from the low lunge position. Then, go back to starting position and repeat with the same leg until exhausted. Then, switch legs. The Kick immediately following the low lunge reception from the push will maximize the plyometrics effect of the drill. This is a very efficient drill. Recommended!

➤

*Powerful push into a low lunge*

### Key points:

- Your partner must push you powerfully but *smoothly* and not unexpectedly.
- Let yourself *relax* when pushed.
- Reception yourself *as far and as low as possible*; make use of the energy of the push.
- *Minimize ground time in lunge position*, whether you kick or not.

The "little brother" of this drill is the Lateral Lunge Push presented in the coming Figures. The methodology and principles stay the same; in the 'extended version', you will deliver a front-leg Side Kick from the deep side lunge position.

*The lateral pushed lunge drill*

## 2.20  Kung Fu Jumps

Last, but certainly not least, comes a drill introduced here to remind the readers that nothing is really new. Many very old traditional Arts included many exercises with plyometric principles which importance had been proven by real world experience.
In old *Kung Fu* styles there were drills like box jumping, or hopping out of a hole that are reminiscent of some of our modern *Plyos*. In fact, many of the "positions" drills or of the traditional forms of the hard styles of *Kung Fu* are definitely muscle-building exercises with plyometrics undertones.  Kicking in series and very low positions switching are great and proven drills.

We present here a basic drill starting from a very low position typical of Chinese Arts (*Pu Bu*). As illustrated by the coming Figures, you jump off the bent leg and switch legs airborne in a double knee strike. You land back in the low crouched position, to repeat on the other side. Once you are familiar with the drill, practice it *multi response!* This is a very complete and strenuous exercise.

*Old traditional exercises are not necessarily outmoded*

# The secret of getting ahead is getting started.
# ~Mark Twain

# CHAPTER 3  BOX DRILLS

*Those drills require a "box" or high step; basically something that you can step or jump on or from. These are the first "new and spectacular" Plyometrics drills discovered by Western trainers in the Sixties, and they are truly the bread-and-butter of plyometric training. The generic word "box" is there to underline that many everyday or specific objects can be used. The height of the box is dependent on the type of exercise or on the proficiency of the trainee. It is sometimes beneficial to gradually increase the height of the box. Plyo boxes are for sale in Sporting Goods shops. But an aerobic step or a stack of those is a good solution to the "box" problem: they are stable and stackable to the desired height. But anything goes: It is the drill that counts...*

## 3.1  On-box Jump in Series

This is the easiest and the most recognizable of the box drills. It can even be done as part of your jogging routine nearly anywhere: on a public bench, a high curb, a low wall...

The classic and unavoidable way to practice the drill is the small legs-together hop onto the box where you concentrate, *not* on height but *on the speed of execution*: back and forth, fast and with minimal ground time. Do not try to jump too high and having then to make huge arms movements to succeed: jump up and down *fast* with arms locked *and rebound on the floor with no pause.*

*Hop on, hop off, as fast as possible*

*Key points:*
- Concentrate on *speed* and *minimum ground time*. Do not try to set the height too high.
- When mastered, *increase height very slowly and gradually* to keep the exercise challenging.
- *Lock your arms* (in guard) to avoid "helping" the jump.
- *Legs together*. Make sure you do not even slightly emphasize one leg over the other.

**The other way** to do the drill is to increase gradually the height of the box. *You still concentrate on speed and no-pause*, but the effort to jump up becomes significant. This exercise cannot be executed as fast as the classic version. This is the reason that the high version should be practiced as an additional drill, but *not instead* of the classic version which benefits are very important to the kicking artist (in spite of the fact that it looks easier and simpler). As an order of magnitude, the starting height of the "box" for this exercise should be your knee.

*Jump up for height then immediately back down*

*Key points:*
- *Height* being the point, you can help yourself with hand moves.
- Make sure you *stand up on the box with straightened legs* before you jump back down.
- *Bend the knees* when you land.
- Work with rhythm and gradually *reduce the pauses in between jumps*.
- Progress *gradually*: this is a challenging exercise for the joints.

**There is a kicking variation** of the basic drill that emphasizes the plyometric angle. From the regular standing position in front of the box, deliver a Front Kick while using the box as a prop to force a proper high-knee chamber. Deliver the Kick as an explosive power kick from the starting position and chamber back. As the foot lands back on the floor, you *immediately* jump up from both feet onto the box, as per the classic drill. Hop back down and immediately deliver a Front Kick, same leg as before. Chamber back, land foot and jump up onto the box. And repeat...

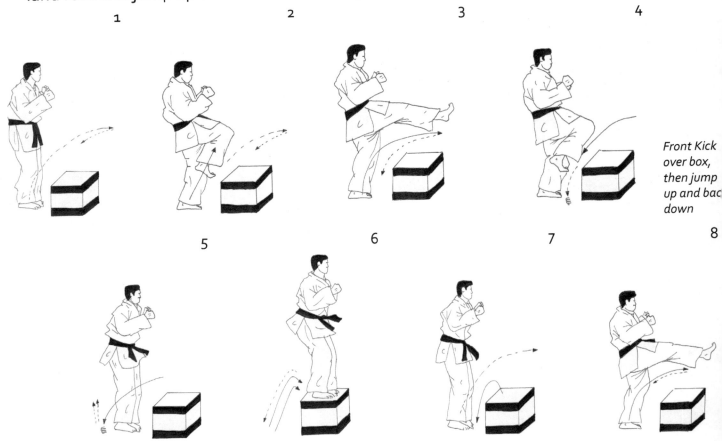

1  2  3  4

*Front Kick over box, then jump up and back down*

5  6  7  8

*Key points:*

- *Drill one leg at a time*; do not alternate kicks in one series.
- Progress *gradually* and reduce ground time as you become proficient.
- The kick needs to be *powerful* but starts from a relaxed standing position.
- Jump up *from both legs* as soon as the kicking foot reaches the floor.

*The front kick then on-box jump Drill*

*Deliver a full-powered front kick before hopping in order to benefit from the drill*

*For all variations, make sure you hop on and off as quickly as possible*

Once you are very proficient in the basic drills, you can start to do **the basic variations** as an additional drill, spicing the routine a bit. The two basic variations are: _twisting airborne_ and _one-legged_. The principles stay the same and we are not going to write too much about it. Just refer to self-explanatory Figures coming on next page. Remember that the drills can be executed in different ways: fast, or high and with or without kicking involved; all previous key points stay valid and should be referred to.

*On-box **twist** jump*

*On-box **one-legged** jump; you can add a kick too*

*On-box **one-legged twist** jump; illustrated with an additional kick*

**Here is probably the right place to say a word about <u>ankle weights</u> and <u>weight vests.</u> Adding weight when doing Plyometrics will obviously increase performance. But it should be clear from all the cautionary words in the Introduction that this is only for very well-conditioned young athletes, and after a very gradual learning curve. The author does not recommend the use of ankle weights or weight vests for jumping and bounding Plyometrics, but for exceptional athletes. Those training aids are a great help though in regular (non-plyometric) exercises.**

## 3.2 Box-on and Up

This is the classic and extremely beneficial drill in which you use the box *as a springboard for a high jump*. This is *not* a multi-response drill in which you repeat the exercise as fast as possible. Instead of minimizing ground time, you minimize "box-time". Starting from a semi-squat position, you jump onto the box with both feet, receiving yourself on bent knees. *As soon as the feet touch the box*, you strive to jump up, off the box, *as high as possible*. When you land, turn around and repeat, but there is no need to run back: Just reposition yourself in semi-squat and repeat. Do not practice on hard and concrete floors.

*Jump on the box and then as high as possible from the box*

**Key points:**

- Concentrate on jumping *as high as possible*.
- *No pause on the box* between the two jumps.
- Only once mastered should you *increase box height*, and not to a point where the first jump is a challenge in itself.

**A goal is not always meant to be reached, it often serves simply as something to aim at.**
**~Bruce Lee**

## 3.3 Box-off and Up

Before we start with *off-box drills*, a word of caution: These exercises are harder on the joints and require a gradual approach. Proceed carefully, and never practice on hard floors.

From the edge of the box, hop off with legs together. Bend the knees when landing and jump up *immediately* from the semi-squat *as high as possible*. Again, this is *not* a multi-response drill. Hop down and immediately up. Then climb back on the box to repeat.

*Jump off the box into a crouch and then as high as possible*

### Key points:

- Concentrate on *minimum ground time after the hop-off*.
- Jump *as high as possible*; try to improve gradually.
- *Legs together* at all times.
- Start the drill carefully and gradually from a low box. *Increase height of box* with proficiency.

The drill is *not* multi-response; therefore, you can cap it with a kick, *immediately as you land from the high jump*. A Back Kick for example, as illustrated in the Photos.

*Land and immediately execute back kick over the box*

### 3.4 Box-off and Long

This exercise is very similar to the previous one; you just jump *long* instead of high. You simply hop off the box and land with bent knees. From this crouching position you immediately jump *into the longest possible jump*. Then, you climb back on the box and repeat.

*Jump down from the box and then immediately as far as possible*

### Key points:

- Concentrate on *minimizing the pause* between the hop-off and the long jump; try to use the momentum.
- The second jump is *as long as possible*; mark distance if you can.
- Hop-off drills are hard on the joints; proceed *gradually* and carefully.

Just like for the previous exercise, you can cap the drill with a Kick executed *immediately* after landing from the long jump. It is beneficial to do so with kicks starting close to the ground, for example the *Drop Twin Roundhouse Kick*, as presented in the Figures below.

*Upon landing, cap the drill with kicks from crouched position like the Drop Twin Roundhouse*

## 3.5 Box Cross-over Jump

This is a very important *multi-response* exercise to be practiced often and always *as fast as possible*. With one foot sideways on the box, you simply jump up and laterally over the box. You land with the other foot sideways on the box, *and jump up immediately back*. Minimizing ground time is the key to plyometric development here.

*Hop back and forth and minimize ground time*

### Key points:
- This is a fully *lateral* move.
- Concentrate on *minimizing the pause in between jumps.*
- You can slowly *increase height of the box*, but only when the drill is perfectly mastered at given height and never at the cost of speed.

*The all-important box cross-over jump*

Once you have mastered the drill, try to increase the height of the jump, while keeping the rhythm.

*When proficient, jump higher while keeping switching fast between jumps*

*Great drill for a fast side-step into kick*

**There are kicking variations of this drill** that are worth mentioning. The *first*, presented in the set of illustrations below, simply adds a Front Kick during the climb up the box. It is a great exercise but care must be taken to keep a smooth rhythm with no pauses. The drill must be approached gradually in order to ensure both good kicking technique and minimum ground time.

*Deliver a front kick while climbing up laterally, hop down while switching legs*

The *second* kicking variation of the drill consists in adding a Side Kick while climbing up. The principle is the same as for the Front Kick version presented before, but it is a more difficult technique to execute. Once mastered, do practice with smooth rhythm while striving to reduce ground time.

*Climb up laterally while chambering the side kick; Kick and chamber back; hop down while switching legs*

## 3.6 Box Switch Jumps

This is a very easy exercise, more like a box-aided jog, but important to do. It is, for example, a great drill to do as a warm-up. The drill will only be beneficial if it is done *multi-response, as fast as possible*. With one leg touching the upper edge of your box, you hop and switch legs as fast as possible and repeat. Continue until muscle exhaustion.

*Switch legs as fast as you can*

**Key points:**
- Concentrate on *speed*. Try to literally stay airborne.
- *Keep hopping* until you feel muscle strain

An easy version of the drill simply uses the first step of a staircase; it is as beneficial if execute as fast as possible and can be done during your jogging routine.

## 3.7 Box Lateral Step-up

This drill is not a jump but a *lateral stepping-up exercise*, great for the knee, the abductors and the adductors which play such an important role in kicking. The drill looks easy, but it is extremely challenging for the knee joint; it needs to be approached carefully and very *gradually*. Start with a low step and slowly; stop at the earliest joint pain. Once you become proficient though, it is an important drill that must be executed in a *multi-response fashion*. I would not recommend its execution with additional weight, but for the most experienced athletes only.

As illustrated by the Figures below, you stand with a box on your *left* and place your crossing *right* foot on it. Lift yourself up straight and let your left foot touch the top of the box before going back down in place. Repeat until exhausted and switch legs.

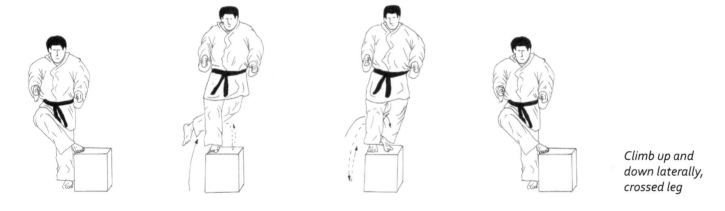

*Climb up and down laterally, crossed leg*

**Key points:**
- Once proficient *minimize both box-time and ground-time*; keep hopping up and down smoothly.
- Keep *upper body straight*, hands in guard.
- Drill with *caution*.

# CHAPTER 4  HURDLES

*"Hurdles" is a quite generic term for basically anything that is not a box. We shall try to give another example each time, but the meaning is an exercise prop that is too narrow or too low to be a box. The box would not be good for the specific exercise, although the plyometrics principle stay the same; therefore a real athletic hurdle, or a belt, or a tire, or traffic cones, or a punching bag will be used. These drills are based on exercises already described but are always multi-response, and the specific hurdle is needed to allow for fast repetitions of the jumps.*

## 4.1 *Successive Height Jumps*

This is a close relative of the Flying Double Knee Kick, with a dash of On-box Jump. This is simply a *succession of forward high jumps* over a series of hurdles. The illustrations show the use of real hurdles as a prop, but anything similar goes: table legs, ropes, belts, exercise benches, ...
It is often done in Martial Arts classes with partners holding their *gi* belts between themselves at the appropriate height. When the practitioner clears at least three of these belts in succession and back, he replaces one of the belt holders to allow him to do the drill, and so it goes... This is a good way to build *dojo* camaraderie.

The drill must be first mastered at a reasonable height and single response. Then, to be beneficial, it must be practiced in series with no pause for at least two, but preferably three hurdles. And back! The height and number of jumps must be then increased very gradually. Starting height should be at mid-thigh.

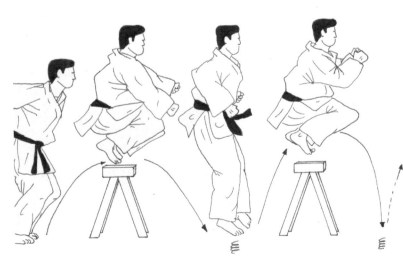

*Jump over successive hurdles in sequence, legs together, no pause*

**Key points:**
- Master the drill *carefully* first.
- Concentrate on *minimizing ground time* first. Not height.
- A series should be *at least 4 bounds* (2 hurdles and back).
- *Legs together* at all times.

## 4.2 Incremental Height Jumps

This important drill could be considered a variation of the Lateral Hopping exercise, made incrementally more difficult. The prop needed is a rope or an elastic band, or belts tied together, long enough to allow for at least three jumps. The rope is fixed from the floor diagonally up to a pole (or held by a partner) at mid-sternum level. The longer the rope, and the more gradual the slope, that will allow for more jumps. Starting at the

ground extremity of the rope, you *hop laterally and slightly forward over the rope*, legs together. As you progress forward, the height increases, and so the difficulty of the exercise. Once the drill mastered, concentrate on *minimal ground time* as you proceed forward.

**Key points:**
- Once the drill acquired, concentrate on *minimum pausing between the jumps*.
- Rope set up should allow for a minimum of three jumps. *The more and the more gradual, the better.*
- *Legs together* at all times.

## 4.3 Lateral Height Jumps in Series

This is again a variation of the lateral hops and jumps. The purpose of the props here is to ensure *a series of jumps with no pause and in the same direction*. This is a different drill than the hop-back-and-forth exercises: Here you keep jumping in the same direction, using the same leg and core muscles.

The props used in the illustrations are traffic cones, but they can be anything that is high enough for the purpose. Remember that lateral jumps are generally lower in height than front ones. Traffic cones are about the good height, but can also be used: stacks of 2 to 3 old tires, ropes and belts, low hurdles, narrow boxes, lying heavy bags, exercise benches and my favorite: partners sitting on the floor... Use your imagination.

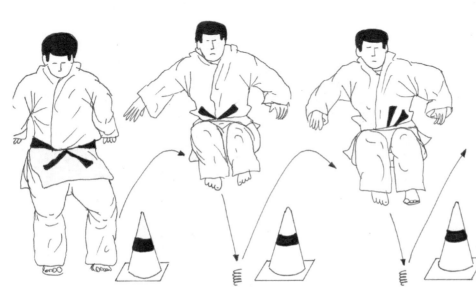

Just make sure you start with about knee-height, and with enough props *for a series of at least 4 jumps.*

Legs together, jump laterally over a cone, then immediately another, and another... All in the same direction and with no pause. Repeat, and then practice on the other side.

*Hop laterally over at least 4 successive hurdles with no pause. Repeat*

### Key points:

- Concentrate on *minimizing ground time* (Make sure props are placed adequately).
- Make sure you are set up for *at least four jumps.*
- Repeat drill several time *in the same direction* before switching sides.
- *Legs together.*
- *Height and distance between hurdles can be increased gradually,* but never on account of the no-pause aspect.

This is a great drill for the improvement of the Flying Side Kick for example.

## 4.4 Speed Side Hops over a Bag

This is a simple variation of the Lateral Hopping drill. The only difference is that the hop will have to be slightly higher and slightly wider because of the hurdle. But this drill is also totally about *speed*, not height or distance. It is also a drill *in place*, with no going forward. This is a great drill if you concentrate on the *multi-response* aspect, and the size of the bag (or any other prop) allows for variations in execution. A stack of old tires can also be used, starting with one, and then gradually stacking a second and a third as progress is achieved. Or a stack of aerobic steps; use you imaginations and the equipment around you. You can also "use" a partner, prone or on hands and knees. Remember: This is all about speed, *hopping back and forth fast and with no pause.*

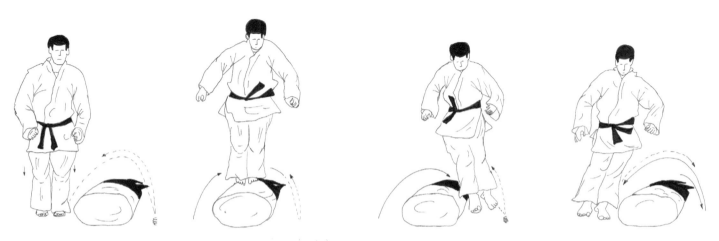

*Hop back and forth over the bag with no pause whatsoever*

**Key points:**
- *Speed*, as mentioned.
- Concentrate on *minimizing ground time*.
- No higher or wider hurdle *before the drill is mastered.*

## You have to expect things of yourself before you can do them.
## ~Michael Jordan

## 4.5 Chair-on Kicks

*A chair is basically a high box with a back. It is also a ubiquitous prop, found virtually everywhere. The seat of the chair will give a plyometric "box" start to the drill; the "back" part can be used for forcing a high and challenging chamber of a kick. We shall present a few examples of drills synergistically mixing plyometrics and kicking exercises, but the practitioner is invited to devise his own as his training dictates. It should be noted, again, that those drills must be approached <u>slowly and gradually</u>: The high stepping can stress untrained joints; these exercises are for well-trained artists in good shape and regularly doing basic plyometric training.*
<u>Caution</u>: *Please make sure the chairs used are sturdy, stable and appropriate for the exercise.*

<u>The Step-up Front Kick </u>is a classic and very beneficial exercise. As illustrated in the coming Photos, it is best executed with two chairs: one for the step-up, and one to ensure a high knee chamber. From a standing position, place one foot on the chair and immediately step up while lifting the other leg into front kick chamber. Kick, chamber back and step down with both legs. Repeat immediately, with the same leg. Once the muscles exhausted, switch sides and repeat while kicking with the other leg.

*Step up and front kick in one smooth move*

***Key points:***

- You do not have to "run" in between kicks but once the drill starts, it must be executed in a *smooth and uninterrupted way.*
- Always go back to starting position *with both feet on the ground.*
- You can start and *familiarize yourself* with the drill by stepping up lower (aerobic step for example) and with no second chair (which back forces you to lift the knee high and early in the kick!).

<u>The Step-up Roundhouse</u> is a more challenging drill, but it will need only one chair as the back of the step-on chair will serve the chambering aid purpose. The principle of the drill is the same as for the previous Front Kick: work smoothly and uninterruptedly from standing position back to standing position, as illustrated by the Figures below. It is recommended, when stepping on, to place the foot turned outwards, in order to facilitate the pivot of the Roundhouse Kick (as clearly illustrated).

*Step up with foot turned out and deliver roundhouse kick smoothly over the back of the chair*

The principles and key points of the drill are the same as for the Step-up Front Kick drill. Other kicks can be delivered as per this set-up: Side Kicks, Back Kicks, Crescent Kicks and more. This is left to the reader's discretion. But one should remember that the purpose is not to make the drills more complex and more sophisticated, but to implement the plyometric principles into kicking drills; the kicks in themselves are, from this point of view, less important.

*Climb up chair*

*Chair-on Front Kick*

*The full Chair-on Roundhouse Kick. Repeat until exhausted, then switch legs*

## 4.6 Split Jump-and-kick over Chair Hurdle

This is an extension of the previously described "Split Jumps" drill (2.16), an extremely important exercise in itself. It is now combined, smoothly *and with no pause*, with a kick. The simple version of the drill only requires to kick after the split jump, and doing so with no pause and with a chair to enforce high chambering and good technique. In the more challenging version of the drill, the kick will be delivered after a step-up move onto the chair.

A picture being worth a thousand words, please refer to the Illustrations below for the Front Kick variation of the basic drill. After the split jump, *as soon as landing and with no pause*, you execute a Front Kick over the chair in front of you. You then chamber back and land the foot backwards, assuming the starting 'Split Position' from which the Kick initiated. You then execute a new split jump and repeat the Kick on the other side.

3    4    5    6

*Split jumps with immediate front kick over a chair*

### Key points:

- Concentrate in executing *smoothly and with no pause*. No need to run, but it must be done seamlessly.
- Adapt the *height of the chair* to your proficiency.
- The drill calls for *kicking alternately with both legs*.
- Advanced artists can execute *with ankle weights*.

The drill can be executed virtually with any Kick and the Artist is encouraged to develop his own exercises as per his own style and physiology. Two more examples are presented: let your imagination do the rest. The first set of Illustrations shows a basic Side Kick drill. The second set of Illustrations shows a Spin-back Hook Kick woven into the same drill.

The key points and principles stay the same as for the Front Kick version presented at the beginning.

*Split jumps into full side kick over front chair*

*Split jumps into spin-back hook kick over chair*

**In the more challenging full version of the drill**, you will split jump *then step-up onto the chair before kicking*. It is basically the two previously described exercises bundled together in series. This is challenging but extremely efficient for the development of kicking proficiency. The Front Kick version of this advanced drill (presented in the coming Illustrations at the top of next page) necessitates *two* chairs: one for the step-up and the other as a hurdle for a high chamber. Immediately after the split-jump, uninterruptedly and from very low, you will step up with one foot onto the chair and deliver a smooth Front Kick over the second chair. Chamber back and land the kicking foot back onto the ground. You then step down with the other foot directly into a low-split (guard) position. From there you will execute a new split jump/step-up/front kick, this time on the other side! Keep kicking and switching sides smoothly and uninterruptedly. ➡

*Split jump low, step on the chair, front kick and back down into low split position to repeat*

And the next Figures show a simple Side Kick version using only one chair. (One can easily imagine a Side Kick forward version with a 90 degrees pivot on the chair, but that would necessitate two chairs like the Front Kick). Use your imagination for more variations). Refer to the illustrations; the principles stay the same.

*Side Kick: The execution is like the front kick variation until the kick itself. Chair is positioned accordingly*

### Key points:

- *Minimize ground time* after the split jump; step up immediately and in one smooth move.
- Step down just as you have stepped up: lower "standing" leg *directly deeply backwards into low split position*.
- No need for extra speed but concentrate on *smooth uninterrupted execution* and repetition. Alternate sides.

And the last Figures show a **Step-up Roundhouse** version of the drill, using one chair only. The back of the chair serves as hurdle for the leg chamber *that is simultaneous to the step-up*. The principles and key points are identical to those for the Front Kick and Side Kick. Work smoothly and uninterruptedly, from a Low-split position.

Split jump, step-up roundhouse, down and repeat on other side

It is now clear to the reader that he can so execute all kinds of kicks and enjoy the benefits of plyometric exercise.

# There is no substitute for hard work.
## ~Thomas A. Edison

# CHAPTER 5　STAIRS

There are stairs everywhere, so it is an easy prop to have and use in your practice. It is a great training aid, not only for Plyometrics: Everybody remembers the movie "Rocky"...

The stairs allow for a combination of both height and distance when jumping. A word of caution though: Not all types of stairs lend themselves to all drills and some set-ups can be dangerous. Always exercise on the lower part of the stairs and proceed carefully and gradually: a fall from stairs is potentially very dangerous.

## 5.1 Upward Stairs Jumps

This is the combination of a high and a long jump, with legs together. You simply jump from the base of the stairs *up to the highest step you can reach*. Step down and repeat. It would be more "plyometrically" beneficial to keep jumping up, but we cannot recommend this for safety reasons. This exercise is also best executed on wide step stairs. One of the advantages of stairs jumping is that is easier on the joints, as you land high at the end of the jump.

*Try to reach highest possible step. Repeat*

**Key points:**
- *Legs together* at all times.
- Proceed *gradually and carefully*. Get acquainted with the exercise and the specific stairs before aiming higher.
- Try to *minimize the pause needed between the jumps* (to get back down).

*Jump both high and long*

## 5.2  Lateral Stairs Jumps

This is a *multi-response drill* in which you should hop back and forth with minimum ground time. Legs are *not* together: it is a Lateral Long Jump Drill (2.7) executed on a staircase. It is even better if you can use a very wide staircase like in a public place, where you can jump sideways while advancing slowly forward with each jump. Standing sideways at the bottom of the stairs, you jump off one leg and try to reach the highest possible step with the other. As the second foot reaches the high step, you immediately jump back down to the starting position in order to repeat. If the set-up allows for it, it is recommended to jump down only one step and then repeat; in this way you minimize ground time and joint pressure, but you keep going up as the exercise proceeds. Something like: three steps up/one step down,...

*Lateral long jumps on the stairs*

*Key points:*
- Concentrate on *minimizing ground time*, but be careful, especially on the jump down.
- *Familiarize yourself* with the drill and the specific stairs before trying for longer jumps.
- *Drill until the muscles are exhausted*, then switch legs and execute on the other side.
- The jump down is not part of the plyometric exercise and is hard on the joints: it needs *not* be executed forcefully like the jump up.

*Jump laterally high, long and fast*

**There may be people that have more talent than you, but there's no excuse for anyone to work harder than you do.**
**~Derek Jeter**

## 5.3 Off-box onto Stairs

In this drill, fully plyometric, you jump off a box *and then immediately up onto stairs*, to the highest possible step. The jump up is therefore both high and long, <u>and after a hop-off</u>; a great exercise, with the added benefit on a jump up easier on the joints. But as with anything involving stairs, be careful!

Do a few dry runs to position the box in front of the stairs at the right distance for your proficiency. Then increase the distance and difficulty *very gradually*. This is *not* a multi-response drill, but do proceed back down and onto the box with no delay.

*Hop off and immediately up onto the highest step possible, no pause. Repeat*

**Key points:**

- Concentrate on *minimizing ground time* between the hop-off and jump up.
- Try to *gradually and carefully* get onto a *higher* step.
- Repeat *until the muscles are exhausted*.

## Our greatest weakness lies in giving up. The most certain way to succeed is always to try just one more time.
## ~Thomas A. Edison

## 5.4  Lateral Up and Kick

This is a lateral step-up followed by a kick. The stairs allow for a higher lateral step-up, and for a continuous exercise (with the same leg) so long as there are stairs to climb. This is an important drill that allows for many different kick types.

As you stand laterally at the bottom of the stairs, you place one foot on the highest possible stair (*Caution: Start carefully from one step only!*). From this position, you explosively lift yourself up on this foot while directly chambering your kick. In the Figures below, the Front Kick version is illustrated. After kicking and chambering back, you lower the foot onto the step just below. You then repeat the exercise without any pause, lifting the non-kicking leg to the next highest possible step. The idea is to climb up two or three steps at a time, each time lowering the kicking foot one step down. 2 up, 1 down; 2 up, 1 down;... Or even better: 3 up, 1 down; 3 up, 1 down;...

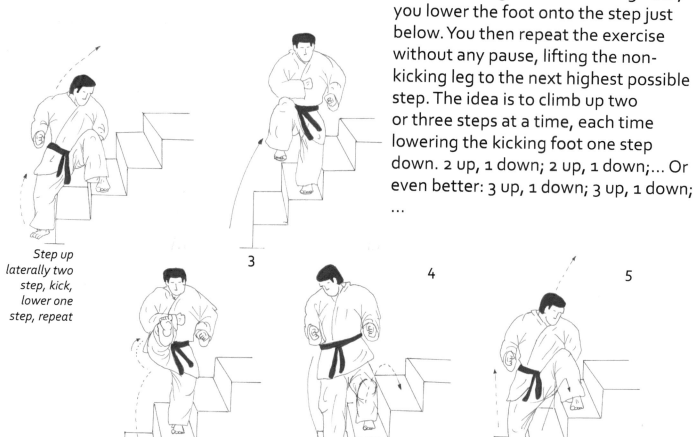

*Step up laterally two step, kick, lower one step, repeat*

3

4

5

### Key points:
- Concentrate on *smooth uninterrupted work, all the way to the top of the stairs.*
- Keep practicing *one side until exhausted*, then switch legs.
- *Start carefully and gradually from one step only; then increase the number of steps up.*
- Go *directly into kicking chamber.*
- When the drill is mastered, concentrate to *minimize ground time between leg down and next step up.*

As mentioned, the drill lends itself to all kinds of kicks and the reader is encouraged to experiment carefully. The first set of coming Figures illustrates a Side Kick version. The second set of Drawings illustrates the drill with a full Roundhouse delivered to the side (no pivot).

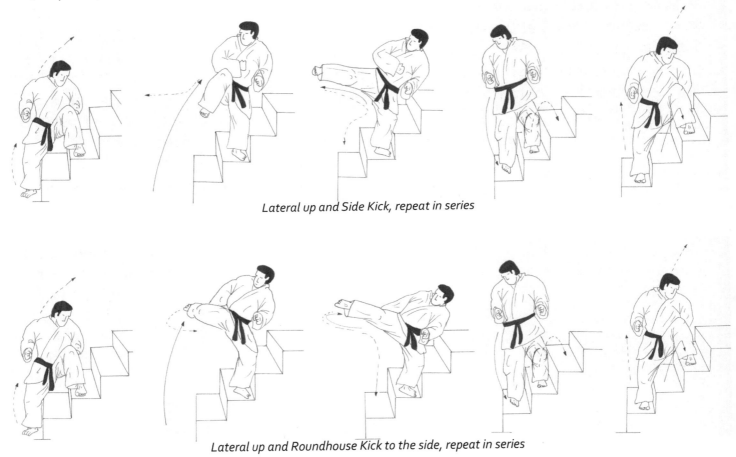

*Lateral up and Side Kick, repeat in series*

*Lateral up and Roundhouse Kick to the side, repeat in series*

The Crescent Kicks can benefit very much from these drills. Many other kicks can be drilled but showing more would be unnecessary. See below. Let your imagination run wild. Try them!

*Stairs Lateral Up and Front Kick*

*Stairs Lateral Up and Crescent Kick*

*Stairs Lateral Up and Roundhouse Kick*

**Every ceiling, when reached, becomes a floor, upon which one walks as a matter of course and prescriptive right.**
**~Aldous Huxley**

*Stairs Lateral Up and Side Kick*

## 5.5 Box Switch Jumps (revisited)

As mentioned in section 3.6, the Box Switch Jumps Drill can be executed *at the bottom of a staircase.* Refer to previous section.

*Box Switch Jumps at the bottom of a staircase*

It is not enough to take steps which may some day lead to a goal; each step must be itself a goal and a step likewise.
~Johann Wolfgang von Goethe

# Chapter 6: Elastic bands, Medicine Balls and Weight Plates

*Elastic Bands* *are a must-have training prop for the Martial Artist. There are several exercise types that are especially suitable for the kicker that we shall present. Most elastic band drills have a certain amount of "plyometry" built-in when they are executed in series with minimum pause. Not all are fully "plyometric", but definitely all are beneficial. They should be part of every kicking artist's routines. A single word of caution: Beware of the band tearing during a drill! One should get a taste of being hit full force with a tearing band to understand the amount energy built-in and the bruising and damage it can cause; the least would be a big blue ecchymosis. It is recommended to discard bands showing signs of tear and wear.*

*Medicine Balls*, *also known as exercise balls or fitness balls, are heavy balls for specific fitness drills. There are many exercises possible, many of them plyometric in nature. Medicine Balls are great for upper body and abdominal development. They also can be used for legs development in more complex drills, but we shall present here only two exercises, with a partner, for the plyometric drilling of the oblique and lateral muscles. These muscles are part of all kicking maneuvers, but especially important in Circular and Spinning Kicks.*

## 6.1 Elastic Band Kicks

These drills are simply kicks delivered with an elastic band around your waist and pulling you backwards. Those are ideal for Thrusting Kicks, where the hips move forward, as they will improve the explosive power of the muscles involved in the penetration effect. They are also very good for other kicks, like Full Roundhouses or Crescent Kicks, but then must be executed with less pull-back. The only kicks not suitable for the drill are the Spin-back Kicks, obviously. A very important point is to always remember, at the end of the drill (at least ten kicks!), to execute the Kick likewise but without the elastic band to feel the boost of energy that the practice gives to the kicking muscles. Always execute <u>five</u> "no-band" kicks after each series. You should be amazed by the results.

The ideal way to practice is with two partners: one holding the elastic band and pulling you appropriately backwards; the other playing the role of the target "pulling" you in just enough to make sure you try to go a little further. Of course, the partner holding you can be replaced by tying the band to the wall, to an exercise ladder or to a door. This will eliminate the fine tuning of the exercise where your partner pulls back just enough to let you thrust forward with effort. But it is good enough for the drill if you make sure you start from a distance stretching the band just enough.

Likewise, the "target partner" can be simply imagined or replaced by a heavy bag or another target. Again, it will not have the "luring" effect of a moving partner, but the extra mile will be left to your concentration and imagination.

The simplest example and most common drill is the straight forward Front Kick, illustrated here with two partners. Repeat at least ten times (or until exhausted) with the same leg, drop the band and execute "free-style" (same leg) five times. Switch legs and repeat.

Some coaches also do the drill with weighted ankles, but I personally think that is overdoing and diverting the focus from the main purpose.

*Elastic band penetrating front kick with two partners*

### Key points:

- Explode into the Kick with no preparatory step or tell-tale. *Avoid telegraphing* your intentions.
- Try gradually to increase *speed and distance*.
- Make sure band is not so extended that you lose your balance. *Keep technical*.
- Always do *at least 10 reps* with the same leg with *minimal pause* time in between kicks
- Always finish the series with 5 kicks *without the band*, at full speed and distance.

The following Figures illustrate the execution of the drill with a Hopping Side Kick while using a "target-partner". The Elastic Band is fixed on a hook in the wall. Principle is the same: execute the Kick as far as possible for at least ten times. Strive to go further and faster each time. Then release the band and execute the Kick five times unrestrained. Then repeat on the other side.

*Elastic band front leg side kick with one partner*

And the next Drawings illustrate the drill with a rear-leg Crescent Kick to a focus pad held by a partner. Of course, the target could be fixed (like a heavy bag or a punching ball), but a good partner will always be better at getting the most out of you. The principles and the way to execute stay the same as for the previous kicks.

*Elastic band rear-leg crescent kick to focus pad*

**Many other kicks are suitable; use your imagination and start drilling.**

*Elastic band-restrained front kick*

**Front-leg** *front kick with elastic band resistance*

## 6.2 Steps and Runs

These are the more classic exercises which purpose is allowing you to move faster to close the distance or to better position yourself for a kick.

The most common of Elastic Band drills, used by coaches in many other sport disciplines, is the Elastic Band *Sprint*.

As illustrated below, you run forward while a partner pulls back on the elastic band around your waist. Your partner uses his body weight and pulls back just enough to allow you to progress slowly forward. You should sprint for ten to twenty seconds, and then come back to your starting point to catch your breath back. Aim to repeat ten times. Some athletes prefer to use two elastic bands and have them holding their chest diagonally, criss-crossed. Up to you...

*Sprint with elastic band*

### Key Points:

- *Partner sensitivity* is key to the drill: You should be pulled back just enough to make the forward sprint difficult, but not to stop you. Your partner slows you down but walks behind you to avoid overstretching of the band and to avoid slowing you too much.

- Make sure you are *bent forward* to make the drill about the legs, and not about the lower back.

This drill is a must practice for *stamina and muscle power*. But, on top of it, the **more Martial Arts-specific versions** should be drilled. Those are basically the **stepping techniques** specific to your art or to your fighting style. We shall give a few examples, but you should drill the specific ones you use in general practice.

Here is the place to underscore how important these drills are! A young artist could be looking down upon these exercises as not challenging or not interesting enough; he would be doing a serious mistake! Maybe not sexy. But the experienced fighter knows that it is the positioning, the timing and all the preparation that will make a technique successful, *not* the technique itself. Learn to move fast first, and your kicks will score!

*The Elastic Band Full Step* is the classic full step forward of traditional Martial Arts, with an elastic band pulling you back. This drill must be executed with an experienced partner who will not be trying to hold you back, but will be exerting just enough force to make your progression difficult. This is a much easier "pull-back" than for the Sprint version. Ideally, you should be allowed to do two full steps before going back to starting position and repeat. Keep drilling until your muscles are exhausted. When proficient, you can execute a classical punch with each step, for form.

*Full Step traditional punch
with elastic band pull-back*

## Key Points:

- The step must be *technically good*: Make sure your head stays at level during all of the step, and your body stays straight.
- Use your *legs and hips*.
- Do not pause between the two steps, and alternate side of first step.

**The Elastic Band Half-Step** is much more important to practical fighting. It will improve your speed of positioning and of closing the gap. As illustrated inthe Figures below, you just push forward from the back leg (in fighting stance) to move the front leg forward up to half the distance between your legs. You then pull in the back leg to get back into fighting stance. Repeat fast, progressing forward without moving anything else than your legs. Your partner pulls back while you execute ten steps in series. Go back to the starting position and repeat until your muscles are exhausted. Then do a five-steps series without the elastic band, trying to make the longest and most explosive half-steps possible. Then repeat on the other side.

*Move forward with exploding half-steps against band pull-back*

**Key points:**

- Concentrate on the step being *your closing the distance* for an attack.
- Make sure that *your head stays level* and that you *do not telegraph* the step in any way.
- Repeat *in series*. No pause.
- Always execute a few times *with no band*, at the end of the drill.

**The Elastic Band Side Cross Step** is a great drill of the traditional side step that will build powerful specific muscles. <u>Do practice it</u>, even if you think the step itself is outmoded in modern fighting. And you should practice <u>both ways</u> to cross step: crossing *in front* (for the Side Kick) and crossing *behind* (for the Roundhouse Kick). Therefore, the best way to practice the drill is to do both ways in sequence, alternating the first step. In side stance, with a partner holding the elastic band around your waist, cross-step in front, and then behind. If possible, do four steps before going back to the starting position. Repeat until exhausted, *then execute the drill with no band*. See Figures at the top of next page.

*Progress with alternating side cross-steps against band resistance. Keep head level*

## Key Points:

- Stay *technically correct* in spite of the pull-back.
- Make sure *your head stays level* and you use only your legs.
- Always execute *with no band* at the end of the drill.

**The Elastic Band Side Step** is the more modern version of the traditional Cross Step. The principles are the same and it should be drilled in the same way. There is no front- or behind-crossing in this case, there is just bringing the feet side by side. But still, one should strive to do *at least four* side-steps before going back to the starting position.

*Shuffle side step against elastic band resistance*

## Key Points:

- Make sure you *do not telegraph* the step.
- Concentrate on the execution as a *gap-closing move* against an opponent.
- Stay level, *no bobbing*!

An important Step combination drill is the **Half step + Shuffle**, illustrated in the coming Figures. The principles stay the same.

*Fast half-step to close the distance, followed by shuffle, against band resistance*

*There are many other steps and combinations of steps that can be so practiced, including oblique and backward steps. Do practice those that you generally use in practice, but do it with the elastic band. This will progressively build your free-fighting skills in ways you cannot imagine.*

Elastic band-restrained sprint

*Half-step drill with elastic band*

*Side hop drill with elastic band*

## 6.3 Step and Kick

These drills are the combination of the two previous one, on which foundation they are built. These are the ultimate drills combining the step that will lead to the kick. Again, the many possible exercises are left to the reader's imagination. Do practice the basic drills and then your own preferred kicking techniques accordingly. These drills are more "plyometric" in that **they are a kick after a step,** and **executed in series.** It is important to concentrate on the step, and then on *minimizing the time between the step and the kick*. Proceed gradually.

The most classical of those drills is the **Half-Step to Rear-Leg Front Kick** illustrated in the Drawings below. Your partner will pull you back *just enough* as you execute half a step forward, immediately followed by a full-power Penetrating rear-leg Front Kick. Go back and repeat, about ten times. Execute then five times *with no band* and repeat on the other side.

*Small step forward with front foot followed by rear-leg full-powered penetrating front kick with hip thrust*

And the next Figure illustrates a **Front-leg** Front Kick after 'Half-step + Shuffle'.

*Small step forward, shuffle, front-leg penetrating front kick*

The Drawings at the top of next page illustrate a **Half-step Low Kick** (*Low Straight Leg Roundhouse Kick*) with full hip rotation. In this exercise, your partner must pull back in a way that allows a good technical Kick. It is also recommended you practice this drill with a second partner acting as a target, to pull you in and to allow for a full-powered Kick on to a target pad. *Remember to do 5 kicks without the band at the end of each series.*

*Elastic Band Low Kick with two partners*

## Key Points:

- *Concentrate* on a "real fighting" execution.
- *Minimize pause between Step and Kick.*
- *Avoid any tell-tale* that would be telegraphing your step.

*Half step and front rear leg front kick with elastic band*

## 6.4 Medicine Ball Twists

This is a very simple exercise, *extremely important* in spite of the fact it looks easy. As shown in the coming Illustrations, you simply twist to pass the ball to your partner who, standing back–to-back with you, twists to receive it. He then twists as fast as possible to hand it over to you on the other side. Of course, you have twisted yourself to collect it. You keep this going, as fast as possible, for as long as possible until your muscles get exhausted. Repeat with the ball circling the both of you in the opposite direction.

*Simple Medicine Ball Twists. Execute Fast*

### Key Points:
- Your feet are *stuck in the ground*, unmovable.
- *Minimize "ball time".*
- Work your way gradually to *heavier balls*.
- After the drill, execute a few *Spinning Kicks*.

## 6.5  Medicine Ball Extended Twists

This drill is similar to the previous one, and the principle and key points stay the same. The only difference is that, this time, the two partners stand a bit further away from one another *and twist in the same direction*. This causes the ball to travel in a "8" pattern instead of a circle, and causes the partners to have to twist even more. A picture being worth a thousand words, it will easier to grasp from the Figures at the top of next page ➜

Drill fast with legs immobile!

*A bit counter-intuitive but forces an extended twist*

This drill, and the previous one, are extremely important for explosive spinning kicks.

*Drill for fast spinning Kicks*

## 6.6 Weight Plate Sweeps

This drill uses a weight plate; start light at 10 pounds and increase weight gradually. The drill is a multi-response exercise mimicking a classic sweeping throw technique (*De Ashi Barai*). It is a great abductors/adductors exercise to be executed continuously without any pause. You simply push the weight plate with your foot as if you were sweeping your opponent front leg. Step and repeat immediately as illustrated in the Figure at the top of next page. Do all the room's length and come back by switching legs. Keep at it until muscles feel exhausted. Concentrate on the sweep and keep hands up in guard as if a real-life attack. When proficient, increase the weight to be 'swept'. ➤

*Step, Push the plate; Repeat*

**Key Points:**

- *Do not rest* in between sweeps or when switching legs at the end of the room.
- Push *sideways and near you;* push across your body line.
- Keep pushing with the *leg nearly straight*.

## 6.7 Weight Plate Ground Push

For this drill, you should start with a heavier weight plate, let us say 20 or 30 pounds; and increase gradually. This is a very simple but very hard exercise: Push continuously a weight plate on the ground as illustrated in the coming Figures. Your hands are on the plate and your arms are straight, as in a push-up position. You start pushing the plate around the room, using only your legs. Work with fast steps to make this drill a *plyometric multi-response* one. Push continuously with no pause until exhausted.

Once familiar with the drill, you can make it even more challenging by having a partner using an elastic band to pull you back. Of course, he should pull just enough to make it difficult but not to stop your forward movement. Your partner follows you around the room while pulling you back slightly. You will hate him!

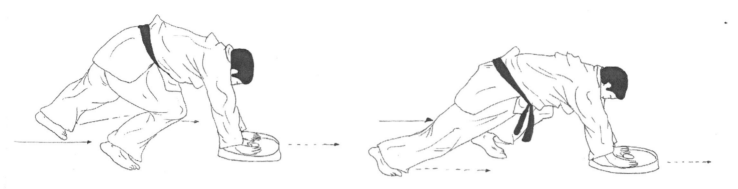

The fantastic Plate Ground Push

A partner and an elastic band will make the drill more challenging

# Victory belongs to the most persevering.
## ~Napoleon Bonaparte

# PART 2

# FLEXIOMETRICS

It does not matter how slowly you go as long as you do not stop.
~Confucius

# CHAPTER 7  GENERAL

## 7.1 Principles and Theory

**Flexibility** could be defined as the ability to use the full range of movement of a joint or a combination of joints and the relevant muscles attached to those joints. Flexibility, or rather the personal "full range" of an individual is very much determined by genetics but can be improved markedly by stretching. **Stretching** is the elongation of the muscles, joints and connective tissues in order to improve flexibility.

For the kicking Martial Artist, the importance of flexibility is obvious: it will allow for longer and higher reach. Hidden, though, is another important, and maybe more important benefit of high flexibility: *Speed*. Even if you kick low, flexibility will allow for a faster kick.

*Flexibility allows you to kick higher... and faster*

**Speed** being a part of the "explosiveness" equation, it is important for all athletic activities. Flexibility improves speed potential. And as Plyometrics are based on contracting a *stretched* muscle, flexibility will also improve potential results from plyometric training.

The other benefits of stretching are common to all sports: better muscle tone, less danger of injury, easy use of the full range of joint movement and reduction of muscle soreness. And the relaxing effect of stretching is clear to anyone who has capped a full yoga session with a meditation and relaxation posture: care must be taken in order not to fall asleep, and the feeling of well-being is great and different from any other brought by exercise. **The generally accepted theory of stretching differentiates between several types of stretching:**

1.    *Static Stretching*: You basically hold a position at its full-range of motion (like the splits). Some authors differentiate further between *Static-Passive* where gravity helps to maintain the position (Splits); and *Static-Active* where the muscles are used to maintain the position (Also called *Active Flexibility Stretching*). Yoga is the embodiment of static stretching, and its results for flexibility speak for themselves. The physiological theory stresses that there is no need to hold a stretch longer than 20 seconds to benefit from it, although 12 seconds is a minimum.

**2.   _Dynamic stretching_**: This is obviously stretching while moving and while using the full range of a joint movement at regular or high speed. It will also usually be in a specific sport application. You basically stretch the muscle dynamically into an extended range of motion, BUT *not exceeding your static-passive stretching ability*. An example is the Straight-leg Front Kick, in which you balance your leg higher and higher, *but not more than the front splits you could do on the floor.*

*Dynamic Stretching: Straight-leg Front Kick*

**3.   _Ballistic Stretching_**: This is the "old" and <u>bad</u> way to stretch. It uses the energy of bouncing motions to further lengthen the muscles and increase the range of motion, trying to gradually force your way a bit further. This has a greater potential to cause injury and does not lengthen the tissues. Do you remember the *Stretch Reflex* mentioned in "Plyometrics"? Bouncing causes this reflex and therefore the automatic contracting of the muscle! Not good!

**4.   _Passive Stretching_**: This is another word for partner training, although the partner can be replaced by equipment and by stretching machines. In principle, you

relax your muscles and let the partner increase slowly and gradually the range of motion. It has the great advantage to allow for stretching beyond the static range of motion, but it requires great care and sensitivity from your partner. Also, the speed of pressure must be carefully controlled to avoid the stretch reflex to set in.

There are more sophisticated stretching strategies, but they are beyond the scope of this book.   ➤

*Passive stretching: The hip joint in Roundhouse Kick Chamber*

We shall not dwell into the physiology of stretching, as it has no direct bearing in how to train besides what has already been written. The muscles are composed of different sorts of fibers, based on different proteins and configurations. Some specific proteins have more bearing to the elasticity of the fiber than others but their names will not help the artist. The joints and connective tissues also play a key role, but most of it is common sense. Most of the connective tissues, that include well-known collagen, are *viscoelastic* in nature. It simply means that, when stretched, they do not revert immediately to their former state like elastic, *but do so very slowly and gradually*. This explains partly why flexibility will tend to decrease if you stop training.

While stretching, the artist has to cause the body to reconfigure itself in a more flexible set-up; this will be achieved by going *very slowly and gradually* a bit further each time, by avoiding the "stretch reflex" to kick in, and by lowering the sensitivity signals sent by the neurological interfaces to the muscles and joints. The only way to do all that is by stretching **SLOWLY**, by relaxing, and by making use of the *Reciprocal Inhibition Reflex*. This is fancy wording for the body's tendency to relax a muscle when the antagonistic muscle is contracted. In other words and for example, in your full stretch, slowly contract your quadriceps to further relax your hamstrings.

## 7.2 Caution

Stretching must be done *very carefully*. It is obvious, as it is dealing with elasticity. Overstretching anything elastic can cause irreversible damage. On the other hand, stretching has been demonstrated to prevent future injuries when done properly, and to have a long-term protective effect.

This book advocates training sessions *exclusively dedicated to stretching*; but appropriate stretching should also be practiced in the warm-up and cool-down parts of regular training sessions. More on that further on.

*Dedicated stretching* should only be done after warming-up, as the warmed muscle lends itself to more stretching and less danger of injury.

Stretching must be done carefully, by "listening" to your body: You have to reach your maximum static range of motion slowly, with relaxed muscles and without bouncing. The position should be held comfortably for about 20 seconds. If you feel it is not possible, it means that you are already too far! More on the methodology further on.

... *Never stretch an injured muscle*. Do not use warming balms (Deep Heat, Ben Gay, Tiger Balm, and others) as substitutes to a physical warm-up; those are excellent for after-training, or in combination with a real physical warm-up.
It will never be said enough: *NEVER bounce or use jerky movements* when you stretch!

*Stretching is no contest*: Do not try to "beat" a partner or friend! Stretching is doing your own best in the framework of your genetic potential, and improving yourself slowly and gradually: You compare to yourself only!

## 7.3 *Methodology for the Martial Artist*

It has already been made clear how important stretching is for the Martial Artist: Flexibility, High Kicks and Speed!
This book refers to <u>dedicated</u> stretching sessions, not to the warm-up and cool-down parts of other types of training sessions. The principles stay the same, with a bit more Dynamic Stretching during warm-up. Any stretch can be done during Cool-down as the muscles and joints are then very warm and supple, but the purpose then is relaxation and light stretching to avoid a shortening of the muscle later in the recuperation phase (especially after power and weight work). All the stretching exercises presented here can be done in the cool-down part of regular training. Needless to remind the artist that Stretching Cool-down is a must after the Plyometrics sessions described in the first part of this book. But a Cool-down session should not exceed 15 minutes.

*Fast and High*

With the exception of Dynamic Stretching that will be treated briefly and separately, the Martial Artist should mainly stretch in the **Static-Passive way**, in the way *Yogis* do train. A few drills of Passive Stretching with a partner will be presented; as those, when well done, are beneficial and do tend to promote camaraderie in the school. They are, in fact, similar to the help provided by the teacher or the props in *Yoga* class.
The constant reference of the author to *Yoga* is not random: *Yoga*, from most schools, is definitely the best way to promote Flexibility. It also promotes core-muscles building, balance, breathing and concentration; and the cross-practice of *Yoga* is highly recommended to the Martial Artist. Unfortunately, not every Artist has the time or the opportunity to add *Yoga* to his crammed schedule. Therefore, this book will present the most important stretching moves for the kicking artist, and whenever relevant, it will mention the *Yoga* posture Sanskrit name.

The drill methodology is also that of *Yoga*:

*After warming up, the artist will take the position described slowly. He will then stretch slowly and gradually close to his maximum. He will hold this position for approximately 20 seconds, while trying to relax the stretched muscles. He should, when possible, try to go a bit further by contracting slowly the antagonists (=the opposing muscles), and then relaxing more. Once relaxed and while breathing out, the artist will try to <u>slowly</u> deepen his range of motion a little bit more, avoiding the kick-in of the "Stretch Reflex". He should try to hold this maximum position for another 10 to 20 seconds. Going out of the stretch should also be done slowly and gradually. A stretch should be executed twice, before progressing to another one.*

Relaxing and controlling your breath will be key to your progress, by allowing you better control of the Stretch Reflex and automatic antagonistic body reaction. *Dedicated stretching sessions of one full hour,* will help the Martial Artist access a higher level. But again, the body needs rest from stretching as well. There should be at least one day of rest between the sessions, and more than three sessions a week is not recommended.

## 7.4 The Golden Rules of Stretching

**7.4.1  Always warm up before stretching.**

**7.4.2  Proceed slowly and gradually.** No bouncing or jerky moves!

**7.4.3  Avoid direct air flow while stretching.** No Air Conditioning or Fan directed to you.

**7.4.4  Do not overtrain.** Full sessions: never on consecutive days. No more than one day on/one day off.

**7.4.5  Do not stretch injured muscles or joints.** In stretching, "No pain, no gain" is a counter-truth. If a stretch hurts, stop immediately.

**7.4.6  No need to hold a final position more than twenty seconds.**

**7.4.7  Come out of stretch poses slowly.**

# CHAPTER 8 DYNAMIC STRETCHING

*These exercises, as mentioned, are more for the <u>Warm-up Phase</u> of any work-out, including Flexiometrics sessions. We shall only present a few drills as it is not the core matter of this book. The moves must be practiced gradually and carefully. The range of motion should never exceed the maximum static stretch range.*

*A warm—up session should be started with an overall warming exercise like hopping, rope skipping or light jogging. The author believes that a subsequent good way to warm up would be abdominal exercises, as they also have tremendous overall benefits. Crunches, leg raises and similar drills will both warm up safely, while strengthening the abdominal belt. Further warming-up can be achieved with regular old-fashioned calisthenics. The author proposes instead to execute slow-motion kicking maneuvers, increasing speed and height slowly and gradually; but this is open to everyone's preferences.*

*Once the body is warmed up, here are a few iconic <u>Dynamic Stretching Exercises</u>, to be performed, of course, on both sides:*

## 8.1 The Straight Leg Front Kick

This is a classic kick in itself. Basically, one throws the front leg held straight gradually higher, and ultimately as high as possible. See the Photo below. Repeat with the same leg at least ten times, preferably without lowering to the ground.

*Front view of the straight-leg Front Kick*

*Straight leg front kick. Repeat without lowering the leg, as a pendulum*

This exercise is obviously directly beneficial to many high kicks.

*A Lotus Kick will obviously benefit from the drill*

## 8.2 The Straight Leg Side Kick

This is simply the Side Kick version of the previous kick. The principles are the same: proceed slowly and gradually with the leg held straight. Repeat, preferably without lowering the leg. The trainee can lean on a wall or on a dance bar for better balance.

*The straight-leg Side Kick drill*

The drill will obviously be highly beneficial to high Side Kicks, especially upward ones.

*A high Upward Side Kick in use*

## 8.3 The Straight Leg Front-back Pendulum

This is a variation of the first kick: when you lower the leg, instead of slowing down, you keep the momentum alive and throw the straight leg backwards in a "Straight-leg Back Kick". You slowly try to go as high as possible on both the forward and the backward move. Keep your upper body as straight as possible.

Straight leg balanced back and forth as high as possible

*Back and Forth*

This drill will be good for overall hip flexibility, but especially beneficial to Back Kicks and their variations.

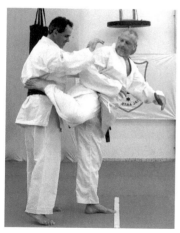

*Some Back Kicks require a lot of hip flexibility*

## 8.4 The Side Knee Raise

This is the lifting of the bent knee to the side in the chamber position of the Full Roundhouse Kick. Lift gradually as high as possible. Repeat, preferably without lowering the foot to the floor.

*Lift the knee progressively as high as possible*

*For faster,...*

*...and higher kicks*

## 8.5  The Inside Crescent Kick

This is a very important kick in itself and the reader is again referred to its classic execution. The Kick is to be practiced gradually higher and wider. The drill can also be practiced with a partner holding his hand higher and higher to force you to pass over it.

*The inside Crescent Kick as a dynamic flexibility drill*

*Kick over a partner's extended hand, gradually held higher*

*A great Kick in itself*

*Crescent Kick Dynamic Stretch - wide*

## 8.6 The Outside Crescent Kick

This is the opposite maneuver of the previous Kick discussed. Everything said stays valid.

*The outside Crescent Kick, practice high and wide*

*A partner's hand will help you kicking higher and higher*

*The Outside Crescent Kick is a very efficient kick*

*Wide Outside Crescent Kick Dynamic Stretch*

## 8.7 The Phantom Groin Kick

Again a Kick, and quite an effective one at that. The reader can again refer to its classic execution and applications. The Kick should be practiced loosely and in a relaxed manner, trying to reach higher and higher. This is a very important exercise, as proficiency in kicking requires a great flexibility of the knee joint that is often under-trained.

*Try to lift the lower leg parallel to the floor*

*The phantom groin kick is a redoubtable strike*

*Phantom Groin Kick Dynamic Stretch*

## 8.8 Cobbler Dynamic Stretch

This is a classic of Martial Arts warm-up. In cobbler's pose, do flip your knees up and down progressively wider. The *static* version of the stretch will be presented later in detail.

*Move your knees up and down, gradually lower*

This stretch is beneficial for all kicks, but especially so for the convoluted ones progressing along a changing trajectory.

*An important exercise for kicks like the Outward-tilted Front Kick*

*There are many more possible stretches and the experienced artist is probably familiar with most of them. Remember, Dynamic Stretching is mainly for <u>warming up.</u> Intense Flexiometrics call for static-passive yoga-type stretching.*

# CHAPTER 9　LOWER LEG STRETCHING

Lower leg stretching is important for overall fitness and injury prevention. For the kicking artist, it will be of particular importance for speed of positioning and for kicks requiring fast pivots on the standing foot like roundhouse or spinning kicks. It is a great preparation for many plyometrics exercises.

*Roundhouse Kick*

## 9.1　Anterior Lower Leg

The main stretch for the anterior lower leg is simply sitting on your knees and heels. *Yoga's* **Vajrasana**. This is, of course, also the classic sitting and meditative position of most Asian Martial Arts, and should pose no problem for the experienced artist.

Some people are especially stiff though, and the pose can be approached gradually: Sitting on the toes first, then the use of a cushion under the feet.

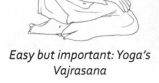

*Easy but important: Yoga's Vajrasana*

*The stiffer trainee should sit on his toes first and then try the stretch with a cushion under the feet*

it stretches the muscles differently.

The trainee should then drill the basic stretch alternatively with opened and closed knees, as

To progress, the trainee should then sit with a cushion under the knees to further stretch the anterior ankle and lower leg. Alternatively, he should pull on his own toes when sitting to stretch these muscles even more. ➤

*Stretch with closed and opened knees alternatively*

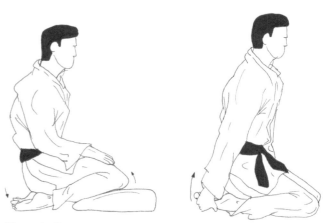

*More challenging: Cushion under knees or pull up on your toes*

*Sitting between the knees: Yoga's Hero's pose*

Once the pose is easy, the trainee looking for a challenge should proceed to sitting *with his bottom between the heels*. This pose, *Yoga's* **Virasana** (or *Hero's pose*), is much more difficult and has the additional effect to stretch the front knee. It should be approached very carefully and gradually.

The next stage would be reclining with the back on the floor to the **Supta Virasana** pose presented later for the additional stretching of the quadriceps (See section 12.4)

The progression of kneeling poses in order of difficulty is presented in the Photos below.

*Progressively more challenging to the Anterior Lower Leg*

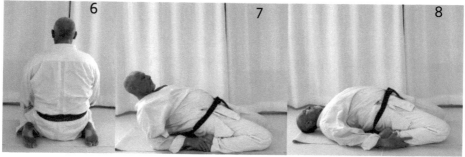

## 9.2 *Posterior Lower Leg*

### 9.2.1 Downward Dog Poses

The Downward Dog Pose (**Adho Mukha Svanasana**), shown in the Figure 1 below, is one of the most recognizable *Yoga* poses. It is a highly beneficial pose, stretching the shoulders, the spine, the hamstrings and the calves. It also irrigates the brain and allows for breathing exercises. In our case, we want here to concentrate *on the lower leg muscles* and tissues, which calls for what is referred to as a "Long Dog", meaning a longer distance between heels and hands. A *shorter* Dog will work more the hamstrings and take off some strain from the arms and wrists. As we are trying to concentrate on the calves and adjoining muscles, it is imperative to concentrate on their stretching, to keep the legs straight and to strive to keep the heels on the ground. The beginner should do a shorter dog, but strive as much as possible to straighten his legs and keep his heels on the floor. With training, he will then increase the distance between his hands and feet for more calf stretch.

The stiffer artist will benefit by starting with an "Alternating Dog", lifting the heel of one foot to better stretch the other one. See second Figure.

1

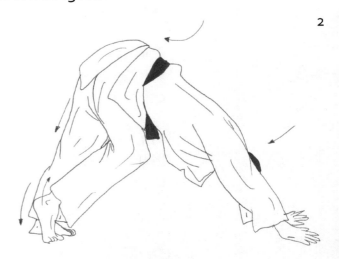

2

*The Downward Dog pose for calf stretch*

*Stretch one calf at a time*

The more flexible artist will try to do a <u>full</u> Dog Pose with all its other stretching benefits.

He will then also proceed to the more intense "One-Leg Dog Pose" (**Eka Pada Adho Mukha Svanasana**), in which more body weight is placed on the one stretched calf. Drill both sides.

*The more intense One-leg downward dog pose*

**Key points:**

- In all variations, *concentrate on the specific muscles and joints* you need to work on; in our case here: the calves' muscles. The longer the distance between your hands and feet, the more the lower leg stretch.
- Keep your *heels on the ground*. Or strive to!
- *Stretch as per the principles exposed above*; twenty seconds and the right methodology.

The progression of the various "Dog Poses" in terms of difficulty is presented in the Photos below:

*From easy to more challenging: Small Dog, Big Dog on toes, Big Dog, One-leg Dog*

## 9.2.2 Flexed Foot Front Leg Stretch

With your front foot 10 to 15 inches in front of the rear foot, flex the front foot as much as possible while keeping the heel on the floor. Lower you head towards your front knee to stretch. This is also a hamstring and a lower back stretch; therefore *you must concentrate on the posterior lower leg* and keep the foot flexed at its maximum.

This is a variation of the *Yoga* pose **Parsvottanasana**, but concentrating on the lower leg.

*Front Leg stretch: Concentrate on flexed foot*

**Key points:**

- *Flexed foot* at all times.
- *Concentrate on calf* muscles.
- Keep *front leg straight*.

## 9.3 Back-of-the Knee

### 9.3.1 Sitting One Legged Stretch

This is *Yoga's* **Janu Sirsasana**: Sitting with one leg straight and the other bent with the plant of the foot against the inner thigh of the extended leg. You lower the chin towards the extended knee while pulling on the toes. This exercise stretches the spine, the hamstring, the back of the knee and the posterior lower leg. Switch sides.

Should the stretch be difficult, you should use a band or a towel to extend your reach, as exemplified in the next variation coming below.

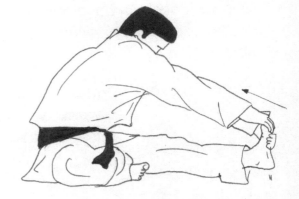

*Yoga's Head-to-knee forward bend*

**Key points:**
- *Pull up on your toes*: the stretch should mainly be about your posterior knee and lower leg.
- Strive to *completely straighten your leg*, then only bend forward.
- The foot should be *flexed at its maximum*.

A variation of the stretch, -especially beneficial if the basic stretch is relatively easy for you-, calls for placing the ankle of the bent leg *on the top* of your extended thigh. This makes the stretch more difficult while also stretching the muscles of the bent leg. It is recommended to begin gradually, with the aid of a band or a towel to extend your reach, as shown in the Figures. Again, *concentrate on pulling on your toes*, not on the spine bend.

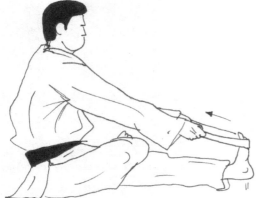
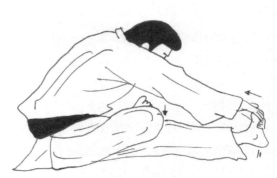

*Ankle-over-thigh forward bend: start with a band*

In those back-of-the-knee exercises, concentrate on pulling on the toes!

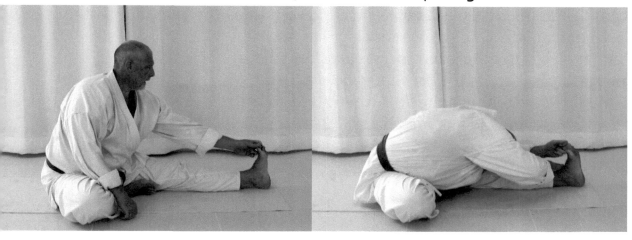

*For Back-of-the-knee stretch, concentrate on pulling on the toes*

### 9.3.2 Sitting Two Legged Stretch

*Yoga's* iconic **Paschimottanasana** is the natural continuation of the previous stretches, bending now over both extended legs. Again, do concentrate *on pulling on the toes*, as we are trying to stretch the back of the knee. And do proceed gradually, with the help of props if necessary.

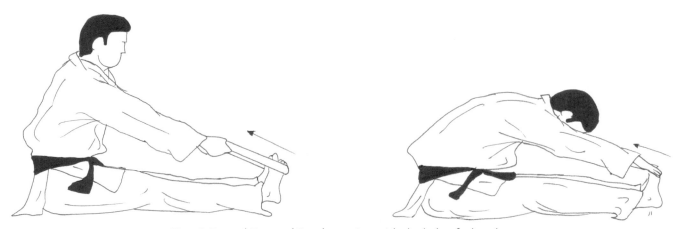

*Yoga's Seated Forward Bend, starting with the help of a band*

The key points are the same as for the one-legged versions. Remember especially the pulling on the toes.

*Bend by pulling on your toes*

### 9.3.3 Crossed-legged Standing Forward Bend

This is a variation of *Yoga's* **Uttanasana** that concentrates on the back of the knee. *It is a very important drill.* You simply cross your legs in standing position, and then bend forward as much as possible. The crossing of the legs will cause the rear leg to be extended at its maximum. Strive to touch the floor, then bring your head to your forward knee. Maintain the position as per our guidelines. Switch **legs**.

*Cross straight legs and bend!*

***Key points:***

- Feet *flat on the floor*.
- *Legs straight*.
- *Concentrate* on the posterior muscles of the rear leg.

*Cross straight legs and bend forward*

### 9.3.4 Lying One Legged Stretch

This is *Yoga's* **Supta Padangusthasana**. Lying on your back with both legs straight, you simply pull on the toes of one leg in order to bring it towards your face. *The other leg stays straight on the floor.* Proceed gradually, starting with a band or a towel around your toes. Switch legs.

➤

*Yoga's Reclining Big Toe Pose, starting gradually*

### Key points:

- Pull on your toes with the foot *flexed at its maximum*.
- Upper body and other leg *stay in contact with the floor*.
- Both legs *fully straightened*.

Remember that Back-of-the-knee Stretch requires flexed foot and pulling on the toes.

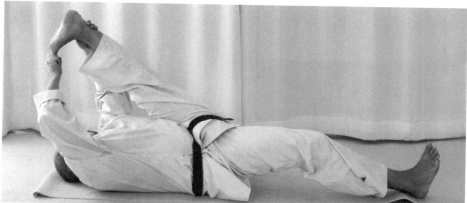

*Pull on your toes while pulling the leg to you*

## I am always doing things I can't do. That is how I get to do them.
## ~Pablo Picasso

# Chapter 10   Hamstrings Stretching

*It is obvious to the experienced artist that a flexible hamstring will allow for high and fast kicking, especially of straight kicks. The hamstring stretches do also elongate the lower back and are probably the most recognizable stretching exercises for all sports. Their benefits for general fitness are many and cannot be under-stressed.*

*Fast High Kicks require flexible hamstrings*

## 10.1  Sitting bends

### 10.1.1  One Legged Sitting Bends

This is, again *Yoga's* **Janu Sirsasana**, but this time with the emphasis on stretching the hamstring. Refer to section 9.3.1 and assume the same position. But in this version, you will not forcefully flex the foot and you will not catch your toes. In fact, the opposite is true: you will try to relax the foot, so as to concentrate on the rear upper thigh when stretching. Bend forward, while trying to reach your knee with your chin; and strive to catch your foot, or better your *heel*. Not the toes. If you can, just place your forearms on the ground on both sides of your extended leg.

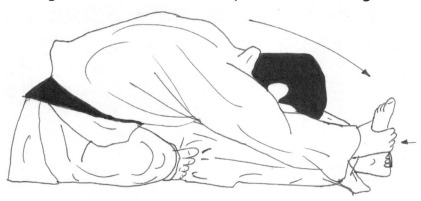

If you are stiff and have difficulties, you can use a band to catch your foot and pull yourself in, but the band should be around the heel, not the toes. Better even, have a partner help you as illustrated, in the passive assisted version of the drill.

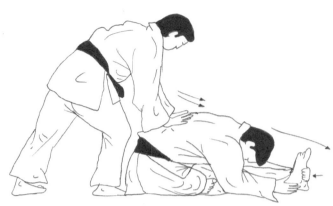

*Yoga's Janu Sirsasana. Start gradually with a partner help if necessary*

## Key points:

- *Do not pull on your toes*, as it will limit the hamstring stretch. This is a different stretch. Relax the feet and pull on the heels (See Photo).
- *Elongate your spine* as you bend down; try to reach not only down but far.
- *Concentrate on the hamstring* and make sure you feel its stretch.

*Do not pull on your toes, but your heel*

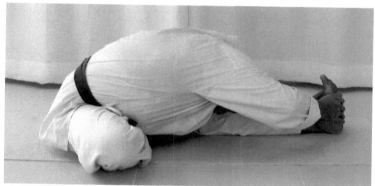

### 10.1.2 Two Legged Sitting Bends

This is now the classic *Yoga* pose **Paschimottanasana**, with emphasis,-this time-, on the hamstring stretch, not on the toes. Refer to section 9.3.2 and previous 10.1.1. Sitting with extended legs, bend forward and strive to reach the knees with your chin. Pull on your lower legs, ankles or feet if necessary, *but not on your toes*. Keep your feet relaxed and concentrate on the hamstring stretch. Exhale and tuck your belly in for more reach. Like in the previous exercises, use a band or a partner to help you gradually improve.

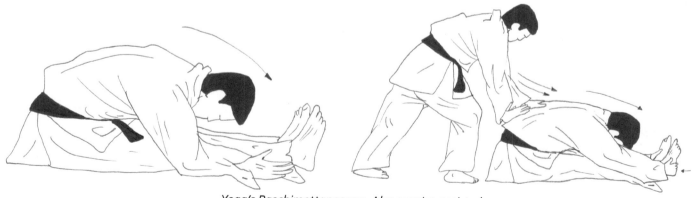

*Yoga's Paschimottanasana. Also passive assisted*

**HAMSTRINGS STRETCHING** 125

**Key Points:**
- *Feet relaxed*, not flexed.
- Legs completely *straight* and together.
- *Elongate the spine* as you bend down.

*Do not pull on your toes, but the heels or the plants of the feet*

### 10.1.3 Open-legged Sitting Bends

This is *Yoga's* **Upavistha Konasana**, the open-legged version of the previous stretch.

This is a great stretch in which the belly does not limit the range of the stretch as it is not hindered by the thighs. Sitting on the floor with the legs opened, you simply bend towards the floor, striving to reach the floor with the chin, as far as possible. As per your personal preferences, your hands could help "pulling" on the floor in front of you, as illustrated, or "push" from the feet. The more flexible trainees will strive to place the whole upper body in contact with the floor.

*Yoga's Upavistha Konasana. Reach as far as possible between your straight legs*

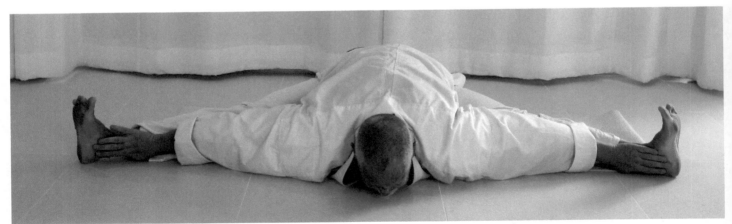

*Strive to place your whole upper body in contact with the floor*

**Key Points:**

- *Legs straight* and feet relaxed.
- Open legs *as wide as naturally possible*, but without stretching out more, in order to concentrate on the hamstring. Stretching wider will also stretch the adductors which we do not emphasize now.
- *Lengthen your spine* as you bend down.

## 10.2  Lying Leg Pulls

This is, again, simply the "hamstring version" of the previously encountered *Supta Padangusthasana* of Yoga. Please refer to section 9.3.4. This time though, you will pull on the ankle or the heel of the stretched leg, *not the toes*. Lying down on your back, you so will strive to pull in the knee of one leg towards your nose. You must keep your back and the other leg *straight and on the floor*. Switch sides.

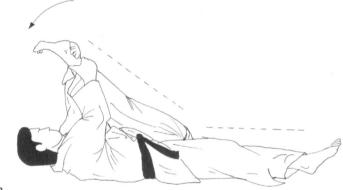

*Yoga's Supta Padangusthasana. Pull in the straight leg to your nose*

**Key points:**

- Both legs must be *totally straight*.
- Back and second leg must be *on the floor at all times*.
- Do *not* lift the head or curve the back.

If you are stiff, it is recommended you proceed gradually and carefully: **a)** Pull the straightened leg in, *but with the other leg bent*, as shown in the first Figure at the top of next page.  **b)** *Use a band* to pull the leg in, as shown in the second Figure.  **c)** Have a partner assist you in passive stretching, as shown in the third Figure.

➤

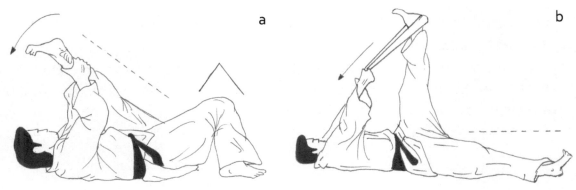

*Proceed gradually and carefully into the stretch*

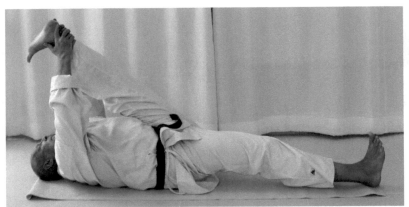

*Pull on the heel, not the toes*

## 10.3  Standing Elevated One-legged Bends

This is a classic relaxing hamstring stretch widely used by joggers and bicycle enthusiasts. You will execute it with more intent and concentration to elongate your hamstrings. With one leg elevated on a table, dancing bar or other prop, or even held by a partner, you bend down towards your straightened knee. Make sure *both legs are totally straight* and adjust the leg elevation to your proficiency. Switch legs.

*Strive to place your chin onto your elevated knee*

**Key points:**

- *Both legs straight.*
- *Elongate spine* as you bend down.
- The standing leg should be about *vertical* for this stretch. Do not go for a splits-like position; if easy, you should elevate the leg more.

## 10.4  Standing Front Bends

### 10.4.1 Front leg bends

*Yoga's Parsvottanasana* is the simple bending over the straightened front leg. Simple it seems, but a great hamstring stretch it is. Switch legs.

**Key Points:**

- Both legs are *straight.*
- *Elongate your spine* as you bend down.
- *Concentrate* on your hamstrings.

*Strive to place chin on knee of straightened front leg*

There are variations of the pose with different placement of the arms. You can place the back of the hands on the floor as far as possible rearwards (See Figure). You can also interlace your fingers behind the back and lift the arms as high as possible.

*Yoga's Parsvottanasana*

## 10.4.2 Classic Front Bends

*Yoga's* iconic *Uttanasana*, concentrating on the hamstrings, not the lower leg.

### Key Points:
- Legs totally *straight*.
- Catch your ankles and *pull in*.
- *Elongate spine* as you bend down.
- *Concentrate* on hamstrings.
- *Breathe* while stretching.

Here are the drills recommended to gradually achieve **Uttanasana**:

**a.** Strive to touch the floor with your *fingers* (then hands) while keeping the legs and back straight

**b.** Place your *hands on the floor, with knees bent.* Gradually straighten your legs while keeping the palms of the hands on the floor.

**c.** Execute the pose with the *hands on the floor.*

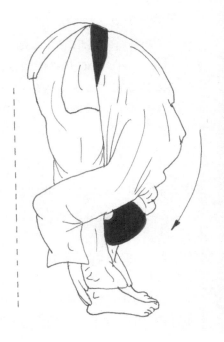

*Yoga's Uttanasana*

*Achieve the full Uttanasana gradually with intermediate postures*

## 10.4.3 Open Legs Front Bends

*Yoga's Prasarita Padottanasana.* Bending forward with wide-open legs.

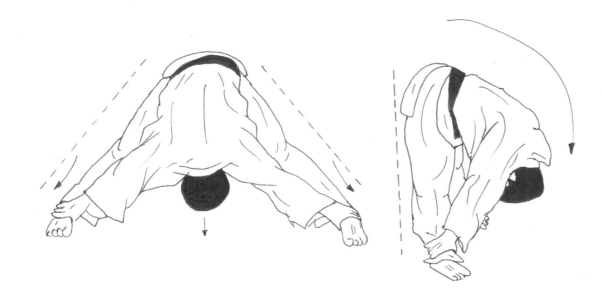

*Legs wide open, bend forward in between and pull yourself down*

**Key Points:**

- Legs *straight*.
- *Concentrate* on the hamstrings.
- *Elongate the spine* and strive to reach the floor with the top of your head.

## 10.5  Front Splits

The Front Splits are an iconic difficult pose that can serve *as a goal to strive to reach*. The *Yoga* version is called *Hanumanasana*. Its importance for high kicking is obvious, less so its importance to <u>fast</u> kicking. The pose stretches much more than the hamstrings, and it is important to *concentrate* on the hamstrings of the front leg for progress in the drill. The Front Splits also stretch, among others, the adductors and the quadriceps of the rear leg; they are a very complete exercise.

The position to achieve is illustrated in the Figure at the top of next page. Proceed very gradually and carefully, using your hands on the floor to control the stretch: this is a difficult and dangerous exercise.

➤

*The Front Splits: Yoga's Hanumanasana*

Once you can routinely take the position easily, it is time for more challenge. The first Figure below shows how you should bend forward and aim your chin towards your extended knee for more hamstring stretch. The second Figure shows the use of a cushion to elevate the front leg a bit more, for even more hamstring stretch. Proceed carefully.

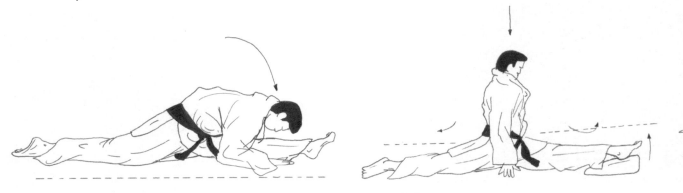

*More challenging Front Splits*

*Use your hands to control your careful descent into the spilts*

## 10.6 Assisted Standing Splits

This is a classic Martial Arts stretch, commonly practiced in many schools. This is not fully a passive stretch, but more of an assisted partially active stretch: You do some of the stretching yourself, though with the help of an experienced partner. There are two ways to execute the drill and you should work out both.

### 10.6.1 Upward Assisted Standing Splits
With one foot on your partner's shoulder, or in the crook of his arm if you are stiffer,

you let him retreat slowly while your other foot stands in place. Bend over your straightened leg, keeping hold of your partner at all times. All stretching principles apply: Take the position slowly and gradually, then hold it for 20 seconds. Release slowly.

*The classic Upward Assisted Standing Splits*

**Key Points:**
- Both legs perfectly *straight*.
- The elevated leg is turned perfectly *straight, knee pointing upwards*, for hamstring work.
- Hold your partner *at all times*.

### 10.6.2 Downward Assisted Standing Splits
In this other classic Martial Arts stretch, *you will bend over the standing leg* while your elevated foot stays on your partner's shoulder. As he slowly retreats, you pivot on your standing leg to position the knee upwards, and bend over. Carefully. See top of next page.

➤

The downward version of the Assisted Standing Splits. Use experienced partner only

**Key Points:**

- Both legs *straight*.
- Make sure standing leg's knee points *upwards*.
- *Use hand on the floor* for confidence building and safety.

## 10.7 Heron's Pose

Heron's pose ( *Krounchasana* ) is a classic *Yoga* pose that also works on balance, but we shall concentrate here on the hamstring stretching emphasis. The fact that the leg is stretched in a sitting position works the muscles slightly differently. Sitting on one knee, with the other leg extended, you pull up the extended leg towards your nose. Refer to the Figure and work with the proper methodology.

*Yoga's Krounchasana*

**Key points:**

- *Do not concentrate on the balance side of the drill; you can keep one hand on the floor.*
- *Bring the knee to the chin, <u>not</u> the head to the leg.*

If you have difficulty sitting on your knee for reasons of flexibility or balance, you can start the stretch while sitting with one leg bent, as shown in the Photo.

*The preparatory version of the Heron pose*

## Through perseverance many people win success out of what seemed destined to be certain failure.
## ~Benjamin Disraeli

# CHAPTER 11  ADDUCTORS TRAINING

The connection between adductor flexibility and high kicks is obvious. There will be no high kicking, and especially no fast high kicking, without adductor flexibility. Side Kicks, Roundhouse Kicks and Hook Kicks will gain in speed with more flexibility. But results will come only after sustained methodical training.

*Flexible adductors are imperative for high kicking*

## 11.1  Cobbler

The well-known "Cobbler Pose", illustrated in the Figure, is called in *Yoga*: Bound Angle Pose (*Baddha Konasana*). It is a very important position for an area difficult to stretch. Use your elbows to press down the knees. The trainee is encouraged to sit in this position, with no extra effort, when he has idle time; just sit. When practicing, the same efforts and methodology as before are of course, warranted.

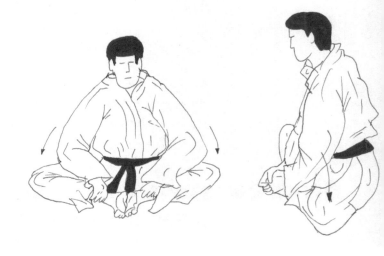

*Yoga's Baddha Konasana – Cobbler's pose*

The stiffer trainee can start gradually with pillows under his knees for gradual introduction to the stretch (See first Figure a). Both beginner and advanced artist will benefit from a partner's assistance (See second Figure b).

Cushions will help get gradually into the pose

The passive assisted version of the stretch

The more flexible Artist will also drill the more advanced versions of the posture: **_leaning to the front_** and **_lying back down._** Those are recommended as separate drills, both in their active, passive and passive-assisted version.

Yoga's Supta Baddha Konasana

If flexible enough, execute the stretch while bending forward

Yoga's Supta Baddha Konasana; execute normally and passive assisted

Aiming to place the head on the feet in Cobbler's Pose

## 11.2 Lying Wide Stretch

This drill is a "light" version of *Yoga's Supta Konasana*. Lying on your back, you lift both legs straight and open them as wide as possible. You then catch your feet, preferably at the heels, and proceed to pull both <u>straightened</u> legs apart and towards the floor. It is important to execute the drill with straight legs; if you are stiff, do use bands to catch your feet as illustrated in the second Figure.

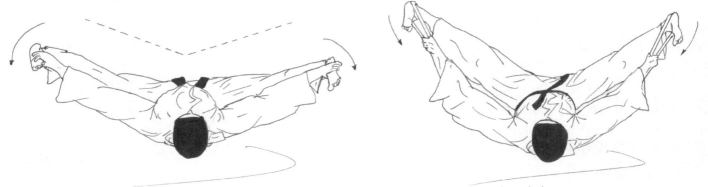

*Yoga's Reclining Angle Pose. Proceed gradually, with bands if needed*

**Key Points:**
* Both legs *straight.*
* The back and head *stay straight on the floor.* Do not try to reach out.
* *Pull the feet* towards the floor.

*Keep your back on the floor; do not go into "Plough Pose" and concentrate on your adductors*

## 11.3 Sitting Wide Stretches

### 11.3.1 Sitting Wide One-leg Side Stretch
This is *Yoga's Parivrtta Upavistha Konasana*, a very important overall stretch. You sit with your legs opened as wide as possible. Always try to go a bit more forward with your sit bones in order to start from the widest stretch possible. Bend sideways, trying to reach your toes with the opposite hand and from above your head. Proceed gradually and carefully, and, in the end, you should be able to assume the pose illustrated by the Figure.

➡

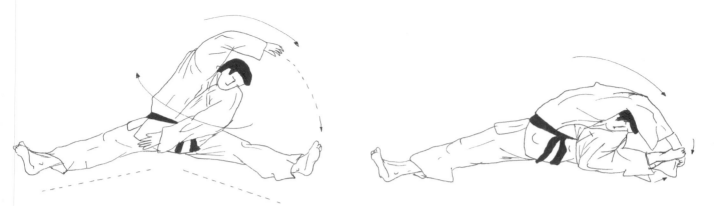

*Parivrtta Upavistha Konasana, Yoga's Revolved Seated Angle Pose. Proceed gradually*

## Key Points:

- Legs straight and *spread as wide as possible.*
- Bend sideways only. *Resist twisting the body.*
- Try to catch the toes *with both hands* while staying fully sideways.

*Bend sideways without twisting*

### 11.3.2  Sitting Wide One-leg Front Stretch

*Yoga's Parsva Upavistha Konasana* is easier than the previous posture, but no less important. It is again required to assume the *widest possible* sitting stance. Stretch open and then bend straight over one of your legs, aiming for the knee with your chin. Both legs as straight as possible! Switch legs.

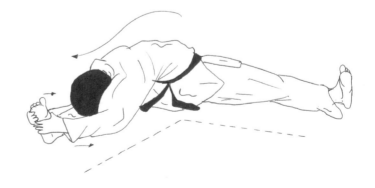

*Yoga's Side Seated Angle Pose. Open legs as wide as possible...and a bit more*

**Key Points:**

- Legs *straight* and spread as *wide* as possible.
- *Elongate the spine* when bending.
- *Concentrate* on the adductors and relax.

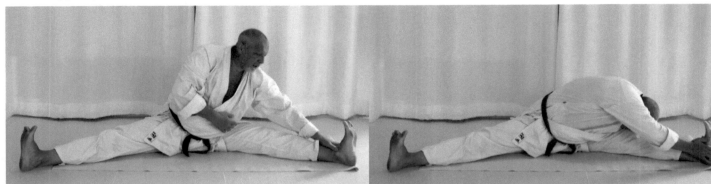

*Elongate the spine while bending down into position*

### 11.3.3  Sitting Wide Middle Stretch

*Yoga's Upavistha Konasana*, the all-important "Seated Angle Pose". This posture is extremely important for high kicking but it requires a lot of training. Sit with your straight legs stretched as wide as possible. Use your hands to pull the sit bones even more forward. Then proceed gradually as illustrated. Bend forward slowly and spread your hands forward to your maximum. Relax and stretch as per our methodology. You should finally be able to lie with your hands spread forward and your sternum on the floor. When you are comfortable with this position, you can then try to spread yourself even more on the floor and catch your feet with your hands.

*Yoga's Upavistha Konasana. Proceed gradually as described*

**Key Points:**

- Legs *straight* and spread as *wide* as possible.
- *Elongate the spine* during the stretch.
- At you maximum, *lift the chin*.

In order to make progress with this very important exercise, it is recommended to get help from a partner. There are two Passive Assisted versions of the stretch very much in use in Martial Arts training halls: Either your partner pushes your lower back down and forward (first Figure); or he pulls you forward by your hands while spreading your legs with his (second Figure).

*A partner will help you progress in the stretch*

## 11.4  Lying One-legged Stretch

Lying on your back, you move one straight leg to the side, slowly and while keeping it in contact with the floor. Catch your heel with your hand and pull the leg up towards you while still keeping it on the floor. The other leg stays straight and in place. The Rest of the body stays straight and on the floor. Switch sides.

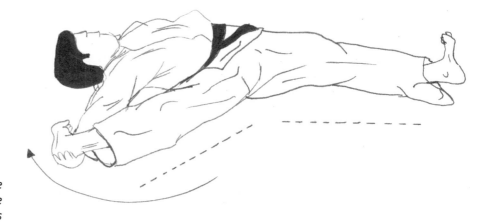

*The Lying one-legged stretch: The whole back of the body stays in contact with the floor at all times*

**Key Points:**

- Legs *straight*.
- The back, the head and the legs *stay in contact with the floor*.
- Try to keep the *body straight and immobile*.
- Do *not* stretch in a way that will *lift the leg from the floor*.
- *Concentrate* on the adductors.

## 11.5  Frog

This is a simple and relatively easy drill: Practice it often and strive for maximum stretch. With the feet pointing outwards, lower your sit bones as much as possible and place your arms between your open knees. In this position, you must already feel the adductors' stretch. You then use your elbows to open your knees even wider. Go for the maximum; it is a drill that lends itself easily to slacking.

*Push the knees open and lower yourself as much as possible*

*Push your knees open with your elbows while sitting as low as possible*

**Key Points:**

- The stretch comes from the combination of the lowering of the bottom and the opening of the knees. *Perform <u>both</u> consciously at the maximum.*
- *Concentrate* on the adductors.
- Try to keep the *upper body straight*.

## 11.6  Side Splits

The iconic Side Splits are the natural continuation of the Sitting Wide Stretches (Section 11.3). Keep moving the hips forward with feet stuck to the ground. *Gradually!* Be extremely careful with this position. The best drills to progress towards the Side Splits are the Sitting Wide Stretches already covered and the Assisted Side Kick Stretch presented later on in Section 11.8).

*Side Splits*

### Key Points:
- *Straight* legs.
- Feet *flexed*.
- Body *straight*.


## 11.7  Assisted Roundhouse Chamber

The "Assisted Roundhouse Chamber" is of course highly recommended for a high or fast Roundhouse Kick, but not only. It is the drill we have already seen in Dynamic Stretching, but executed as per our static (passive) methodology. It is best to execute the drill in full guard and in fighting chamber position. If you are stiff or have balance difficulties, you should lean on a wall, but try to keep as erect as your flexibility allows. See illustrations at the top of next page

➡

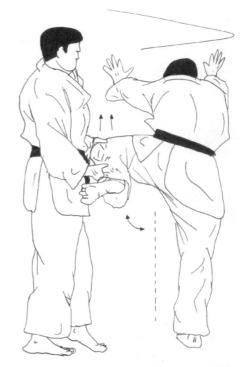

*Your partner lifts the chambered knee. Lean on a wall if necessary*

## Key Points:

- Keep your *upper body straight*; do not lean sideways.
- *Concentrate* on the adductors.
- Standing leg must be *straight*.

*Assisted Roundhouse Chamber Stretch*

### 11.8  Assisted Side Kick

This is basically an assisted standing "Side Splits", but with emphasis on the specific kicking posture. An important exercise to be drilled carefully with an experienced partner. Start gradually with a simple lifting of the leg while you lean on a wall for safety and balance (Figure a, top of next page). You can later place your foot on his shoulder and let go of the wall (Figure b). The position you should strive for is illustrated by Figure c.

a

b

*Proceed gradually towards
standing side splits*

c

## Key Points:
- Both legs *straight*.
- *Concentrate on a good side kick position*; body, hips and legs in line.
- Make sure your partner will release the stretch *as soon as you signal him*.

*Foot on shoulder in Side Kick
Position*

# CHAPTER 12    QUADRICEPS

*Quad flexibility is important for overall speed, for Back Kicks and all sorts of Spin-back Kicks. It is also a very busy muscle in all kicking maneuvers and stretching will certainly promote speed and injury resistance.*

Back Kick

## 12.1 *Standing Quad Stretch*

a

This is a simple, classic, but often neglected stretch. Usually only used as a cool-down light stretch, it should in fact be worked upon seriously and methodically by the serious Artist. Quads are often neglected in stretching routines, undeservedly.

The Standing Quad Stretch is the simple pulling of the heel towards the buttock (Figure a). The feel of the quad stretch is very clear, and it is important to go as far as possible each time: it is not a relaxing exercise but a full stretch by itself. If you encounter some difficulties in executing the stretch, there are two preparatory versions to drill, illustrated in Figures b and c: using a wall for balance and executing the drill lying on the floor.

The Standing Quad Stretch

b

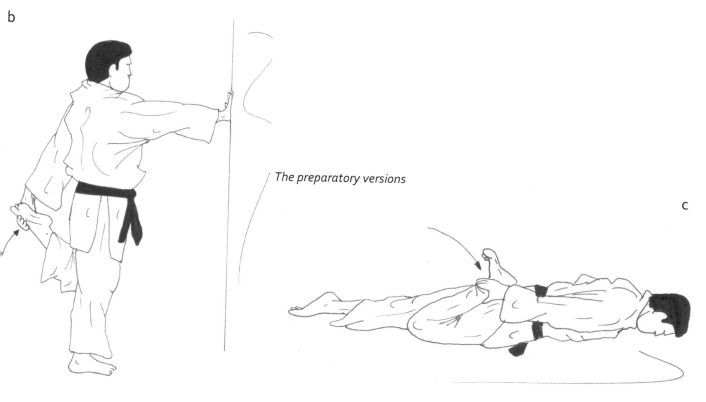

*The preparatory versions*

c

Once you perform the stretch routinely and easily to its maximum, there are three variations you can execute from time to time:

**A.** Pulling the opposite foot, i.e. the left foot with the right hand and vice-versa. It stretches the quadriceps a bit differently.

**B.** Using a wall to push the heel towards the buttock in order to increase the stretch. You use your body weight to go further.

**C.** Using a table, a high stool, or the saddle of a stationary bike to push the foot toward the buttock. The principle is the same as B) , but you lean *down* as well as back with your body weight.

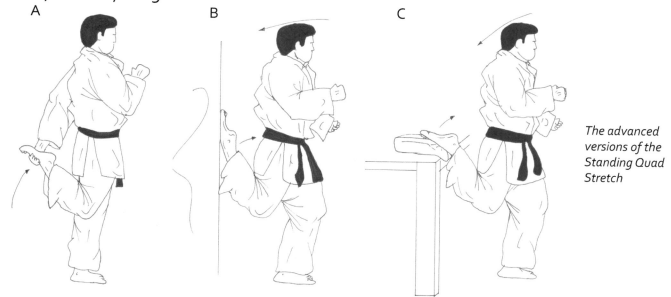

A          B          C

*The advanced versions of the Standing Quad Stretch*

**Key Points:**

- *Concentrate* on the quadriceps, "feel" the stretch.
- Treat it as a challenging stretch and *go as far as possible*, as per our stretching methodology.
- Keep the *thigh vertical* and in contact with the standing thigh.
- Keep the body straight, *no leaning*.

Once you have mastered the basic stretch, you should move the thigh around, as in the coming Photos, for joint flexibility and to look for the position in which you should most stretch in; "where you feel the stretch more!". For example, as illustrated, you can make the stretch more challenging by lifting the thigh back,

*Look for more challenging angles*

### 12.2  Kneeling Quad Stretch

From a one-knee stance, you grab your rear ankle with the same-side hand and pull your heel towards your buttock. You lean forward and deepen the lunge for a longer stretch. The Illustration at the top of next page is self-explanatory. If the floor is hard or your if your knee is sensitive, place a towel or a cushion under the knee.

➤

*Stretch the quad in deep lunge*

*Use a towel or cushion to prevent knee stress*

**Key Points:**
- The lunge, i.e. the opening between the legs, must be *as deep as possible*.
- *Concentrate* on the quad being stretched.
- Lean forward and *lower your hips*.

## 12.3 Reclining Hero Pose

The "Reclining Hero Pose" ( *Supta Virasana* ) has been mentioned in the lower leg stretching section (Section 9.1). It is also an extremely effective, but difficult, quad stretch. It is highly recommended but must be approached very gradually because it strains the knees (The sit bones lie between the knees). But once it has been mastered, it is a great posture, increasing flexibility in the whole of the front leg.
Caution though: proceed extremely carefully and gradually from the simple "sitting on your knees'-pose. The progression, *illustrated at the top of next page*, should be: one-leg stretch reclining on elbows, both-legs stretch reclining on elbows, and the final both-legs back-on-the-floor posture.

**Key Points:**
- *Concentrate* on the quadriceps.
- Strive to place *the whole back* in contact with the floor.

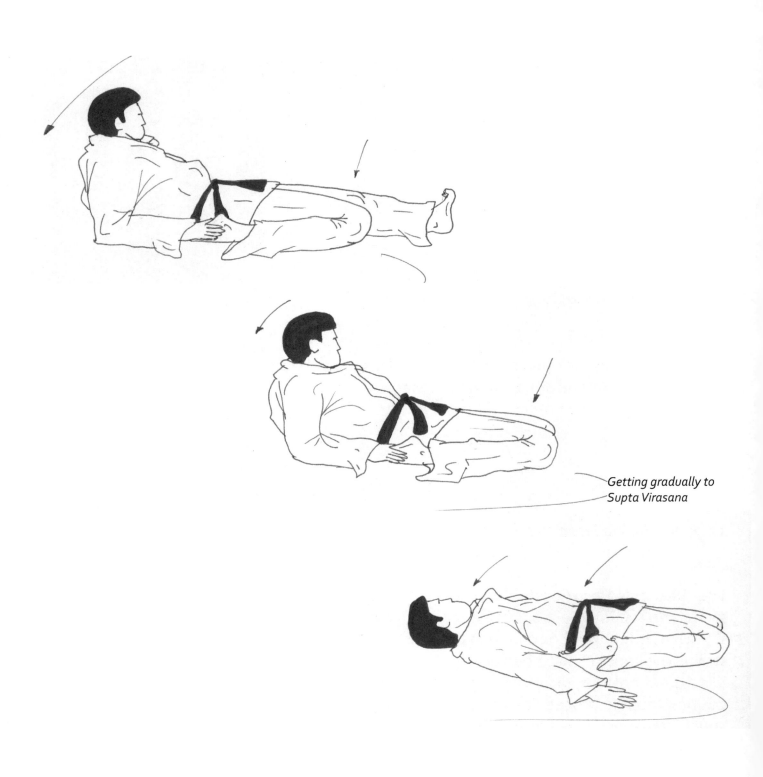

*Getting gradually to Supta Virasana*

**Whether you think you can or think you can't, you're right.**
**~Henry Ford**

# CHAPTER 13    GLUTEI AND HIP BELT

*The buttocks and hip joints are obviously a part of fast and good kicking. Good posture and technical delivery will all be influenced by their flexibility. These muscles' tonus will also be critical in one's ability to position oneself for a decisive kick.*

*A Downward Back Kick, and a good reason for hip belt flexibility*

## 13.1  Deep Step

The "Deep Step", or "Low Lunge" Stretch is very important and must be drilled as a full-fledged stretch, not as a relaxing or cool-down exercise. Called *Anjaneyasana* in *Yoga*, it must be taken to the limit each time, and then a bit more...

You simply take a deep lunge position with one leg extended straight behind you. Push the hips forward and feel the hip joint and the quadriceps being stretched. In *Yoga*, you generally extend the hands over your head, pointing at the sky. In our case, it is enough to let the arms dangle at the side; just make sure your body is straight and vertical and that you do not use the hands to resist the stretch. Switch legs.

*Anjaneyasana, push the hips forward*

**Key Points:**
- Extend the leg *back as far as possible*.
- Bend the front leg by *pushing the hips forward*.
- Keep the upper body *straight* and vertical, or even bending slightly backwards.
- *Concentrate* on the hip joint.

*When proficient, try to curve the back and elongate the spine for a more challenging stretch*

## 13.2  Splits

We have already encountered the (Front) Splits in section 10.5. The Splits are a very complete stretching exercise, putting in play many of the muscles group. There are two ways to further stretch the hip joints presented in Figures 13.2.1 and 13.2.2. Use a pillow or a folded towel to increase the height of the rear or the front leg. Of course, to do so, you need to master the classic Front Splits first. Proceed carefully and gradually. Do not forget to practice both sides by switching the leg that is in front.

*The "enhanced" Front Splits*

*Easing into enhanced front splits positions*

## 13.3  Lying Knee Twist

This is a well-known cooling down pose to be drilled as a full-fledged stretch. Lying on your back with one arm extended sideways, you push the knee of the extended hand side towards the ground, while keeping your back, extended arm and extended straight leg on the ground. It is easy to understand from the Illustration.

**Key Points:**
- The shoulders and back stay straight and *in contact with the floor.*
- Keep the extended hand *on the floor* and perpendicular to the body.
- Use the other hand to *push the knee* towards the floor.
- *Look* towards your extended hand.

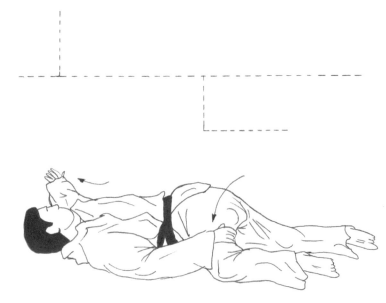

*Rotate the hips, not the trunk!*

## 13.4  Lying Leg Twist

This is *Yoga's Eka Pada Jathara Parivarttanasana*, also a pose often used during cool down of Martial Arts classes. It is an important stretch to drill and bring to the limits of flexibility.

Lying on your back in a cross-like position, you lift one straightened leg and let it fall towards the extended opposite hand. Proceed slowly and carefully and keep your shoulders and back on the floor. Maintain the position while striving to have as much back in floor contact as possible. Switch sides.

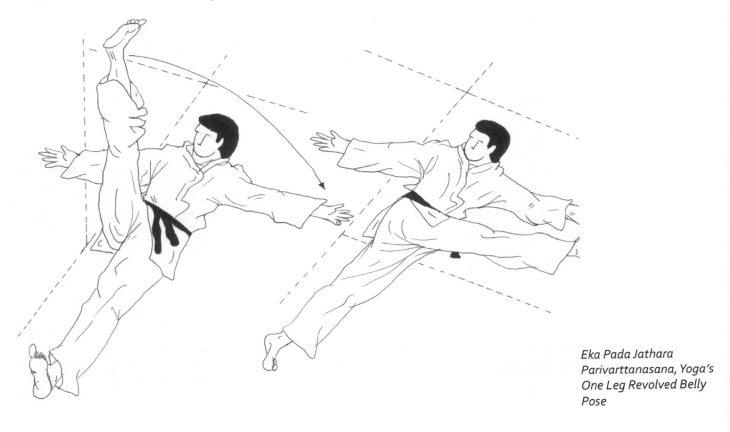

*Eka Pada Jathara Parivarttanasana, Yoga's One Leg Revolved Belly Pose*

### Key Points:
- All body parts are *perpendicular* to one another (See Figure).
- Shoulders, extended hands and back *in contact with the floor at all times*.
- Both legs fully *straight*.
- *Look* to the opposite side of the foot.
- Strive to place the *foot in the palm of the hand*.

## 13.5  Waist Twist

*Yoga's Eka Pada Parivrtta Upavisthasana.* Sitting with one leg straight and the other bent and crossed over the other, you twist your upper body to the side of the bent leg. Use your elbow to maintain and go further in the pose. The Drawing makes the pose clear.

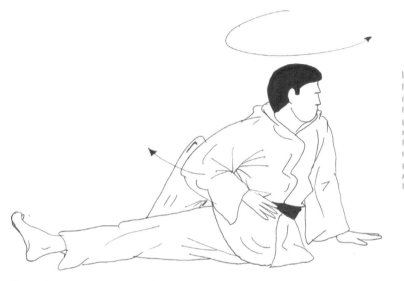

**Key Points:**
- Keep the upper body *straight and vertical.*
- Your sit bones and extended leg stay *on the floor at all times.*

*Eka Pada Parivrtta Upavisthasana, Yoga's One Leg Revolving Seated Pose*

## 13.6  Bent Leg Pull

This is a very simple and natural exercise that you can execute sitting or lying down. You simply pull your foot towards your upper chest or face, like you probably used to do as a small child. The very flexible can aim to place the foot behind the neck. Use both hands to pull the leg in and make sure your back is straight. The coming Drawings illustrate respectively the sitting and the lying version of the stretch.

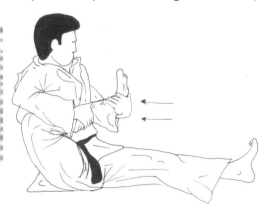

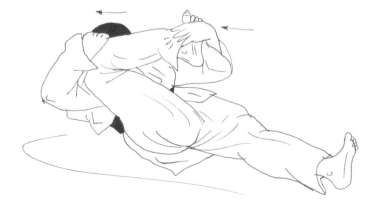

**Key Points:**
- The back is *straight at all times*, whether sitting or lying.
- Do not go towards the foot with the body; *pull the foot in without moving the body.*
- If possible, *lift* the leg towards the face

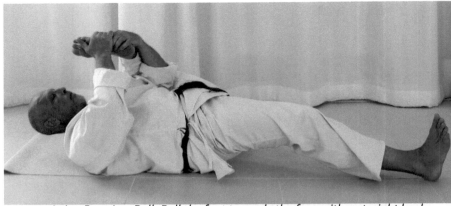

*Lying Bent Leg Pull. Pull the foot towards the face with a straight back*

## 13.7  Runner's Stretch

The well-known "Runner's Stretch" is called in *Yoga*: Supported Pigeon Pose (*Salamba Kapotasana*). The full Pigeon Pose (*Kapotasana* ), -in which the hands are lifted towards the sky and the body curves back-, is less relevant to our purpose.

The coming Figure shows how the front leg is bent, the rear leg is extended and the upper body is straight and vertical. The more flexible you are or you become, the more "open" the straight leg should be, up to 90 degrees. Support yourself with your hands for control of the stretch.

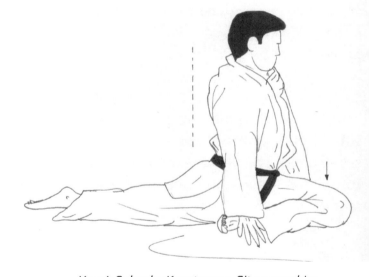

*Yoga's Salamba Kapotasana. Sit on your hips*

Once familiar with the stretch, the trainee should do an additional exercise: lower his trunk to the floor and stretch his hands as far as possible, concentrating on stretching the gluteal and inner thigh muscles. The variation is illustrated at the top of next page.

➤

*Bend forward in "Pigeon Pose" and try to reach as far as possible*

This is an extremely beneficial stretch for overall flexibility and well-being. To be practiced often, but while concentrating on the buttock's muscles and adjoining joints.

**Key points:**
- Make sure *your buttock lies on the floor* and does not "hang" in the air.
- The wider the *knee angle*, the more the inner leg muscles are stretched (and the less the gluteus).

*Runner's stretch: start up as straight as possible; then bend down as low and as far as possible*

## 13.8  Cross Side Bends

Easy but often neglected. It should be treated as a full-fledged stretch and one should strive to go lower and lower each time. You simply cross your straightened legs in a standing position and bend to your side. You are aiming the hands to the floor on the side of the blade of the front foot.  Keep your legs straight. Just for balance, as it is not a hip belt stretch, bend then on the other side for relaxing the muscles. Then switch legs and cross them with the other leg in front.

*Bend sideways with legs crossed. Feel the stretch*

You can progress towards the stretch, or warm up, by doing the bend with legs un-crossed first. Then execute the stretch by bending on the side of the crossing front leg. Bend on the other side to relax.

*Warm up uncrossed, Stretch, Bend the other way for release*

## 13.9 Side Chamber Assisted Stretch

This is a classic of Martial Arts training halls. Just make sure you practice the stretch with the right methodology, as a full-fledged stretch. Go a bit further each time and concentrate on the muscles stretched. This is, of course, a passive-assisted stretch. As shown in the Figure, lift your leg in Side Kick-chamber with your back to a wall. Your partner will grab your foot to push your knee both up and towards your face, stretching a whole set of muscles and joints. Have him proceed gradually and carefully. Switch legs.

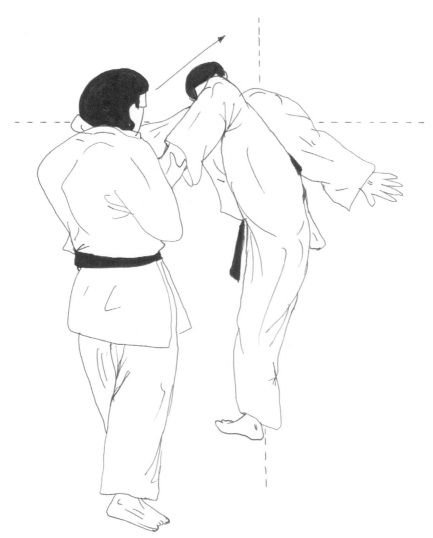

*Side Kick chamber- Passive assisted stretch*

# CHAPTER 14    ABDOMINALS

*The whole body is held together by the abdominal belt. Needless to tell the experienced artist the key role played by the "tanden" of Karate or "tan tien" of Kung Fu. Successful kicking involves the whole body and its maximum use. This will only be possible with a strong **and flexible** abdominal belt. Strong abdominal muscles-building must be accompanied by flexibility training, just like any other muscle.*

*Abdominals hold the body together in all kicks*

## 14.1  Cobra Stretch

*Yoga's* iconic *Bhujangasana*, Cobra's Pose, is a great stretch for the abdominals and the lower spine. Execute carefully.

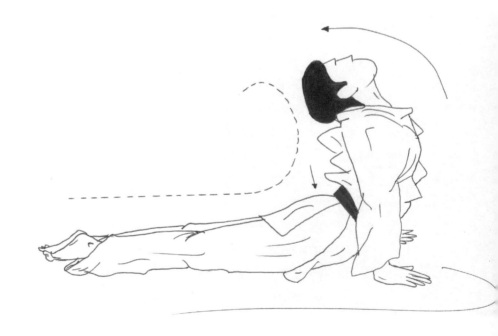

*Cobra's pose. Keep the hips on the floor*

**Key Points:**

- Keep and *push the hips on the floor*; arch the back from the belt up.
- Push on the hands carefully and *gradually*.
- *Look up* at the ceiling.

In order to progress, whether you are stiff or flexible, you can execute the passive-assisted version of the stretch, as illustrated in the adjacent Figure. The key points stay the same.

*The assisted version of Bhujangasana*

There is an assisted version of the "inverted" pose that is noteworthy. Once you are proficient in the Cobra Pose, it is beneficial to practice **_very carefully_**. See Drawing below and execute with an experienced partner only!

*The inverted Cobra Stretch – assisted. Drill with extreme caution*

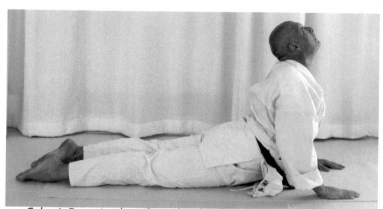

*Cobra's Pose: Look at the ceiling but keep belt knot on the floor*

## 14.2 Camel Stretch

This is also a classic *Yoga* Pose to be drilled seriously: *Ustrasana*, the Camel's Pose. On your knees, you simply bend back and place your hands on your heels or the plant of your feet. Work according to our stretching methodology.

### Key Points:
- Place the hands on your feet, then start pushing the *hips forward* and the chest up.
- Try to *look back*.
- Proceed *gradually*.

*Camel's pose to stretch the abdominals and the spine*

*Proceed gradually from a heels-up position*

If you are not flexible enough, sit on your toes and try gradually to reach the heels, as illustrated in the first Photo. Then gradually try for the plants of the straightened feet (Second Photo).

## Start where you are. Use what you have. Do what you can.
## ~Arthur Ashe

## 14.3  Balance Stretch

*Yoga's* Bow Pose, *Dhanurasana*, is a great stretch for the shoulders, the spine and the abs.  Lying prone on the floor, you catch your ankles with your hands and pull yourself up. You look forward while using your legs and arms to arch your back as far as possible.

Yoga's Dhanurasana, the Bow. Pull yourself up to your maximum

The Bow; pull and look up

### Key Points:
*   *Concentrate* on the abdominal stretch.
*   Open the legs, *not the knees*, for a deeper stretch.
*   *Lift the head* for a deep abs stretch.

## 14.4  Bridge Stretch

This is a well-known exercise, especially by wrestlers and gymnasts, but it is also a basic *Yoga* posture named: *Sirsa Setu Bandhasanasana*. Remember we consider it here as an abdominal stretch and therefore you should concentrate on the maximal arching of the back.

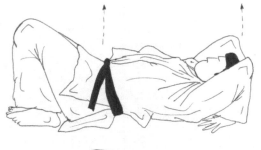

The Drawings show how you lift yourself from prone position on your hands and feet. Arch the back, and then place your head on the floor for the bridge pose (Last Drawing).

When proficient and flexible enough, you can proceed to the more challenging "Upward Bow Pose": *Yoga's Urdhva Dhanurasana*. From the Bridge Pose, you strive to straighten the arms and legs for an extended arching of the back and more frontal stretch. Proceed carefully, with assistance, and make sure you do not fall on the head when releasing.

*Lift the bottom up and arch your back to stretch the abs in Yoga's Sirsa Setu Bandhasanasana*

*The challenging Inverted Bow Pose*

### Key Points:
- Start with hands as close as possible *to the shoulders*.
- Start with feet as close as possible *to the bottom*.
- Be extremely *careful with neck* position.
- Use back muscles *to arch*, not only arms and legs.
- *Concentrate* on the abs stretch; arch as much as possible, including the neck

# CHAPTER 15 LOWER BACK AND LATERALS

*The lower back and laterals are part of the abdominal belt mentioned earlier in the text. Everything said in the introduction stays true. On top of that, the lower back and laterals are key engines in the execution of circular and spinning kicks. The exercises presented below, sometimes neglected, are very important to the Martial Artist. It is recommended to introduce at least two of these Upper Body Stretches into your Flexiometric Routine.*

*Special Kicks are especially demanding for the abdominal belt, the lower back and the laterals*

## 15.1 Standing Bends

We have already encountered the standing bends in section 10.4.2, as a hamstring stretch. The drill is the same, but you need to maximize the spine elongation <u>and concentrate on the lower back</u>. A preparatory exercise, in order to learn to differentiate between the hamstring and the lower back emphasis, is presented in Figure 15.1.1: Bend over your straight legs until your trunk is parallel to the ground; and elongate your spine.

*Bend to 90 degrees with legs straight. Stretch the spine*

Once this is going well, you should proceed with the regular front bends. Please Refer to section 10.4.2 for the bend and its preparatory drills; <u>**just remember to now concentrate on the lower back stretch.**</u>

*The progression to the classic Front Bend*

## Key Points:

- As mentioned, *concentrate* on the lower back stretch.
- Elongate the spine and try to reach as low as possible *with the chin on the legs.*
- Go for *reach*, not bend.

*Proceed gradually and carefully to the full Front Bend*

## 15.2  Plough

This is again a classic *Yoga* pose, *Halasana*, well-known as the ultimate spine stretch. Lying on your back, you simply lift your straightened legs over your head until the feet touch the floor. This is also a neck stretch and you have to proceed very carefully with this area.

### Key Points:

*   *Concentrate* on the spine and lower back.
*   Do *not* try to go further back with the feet, as it sways the stretch towards the neck.

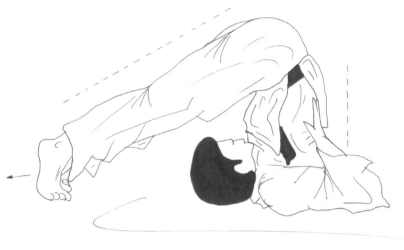

*The Plough. Yoga's Halasana*

The position is not easy and needs to be approached *gradually*. It also restrains somewhat the ability to breathe, and, as such, is a great drill for wrestlers and grapplers.

There are several ways to approach the final pose:

**a.**  Execute **with open legs**. This is *Yoga's Supta Konasana* or the Reclining Angle Pose, although it is usually practiced with the widest possible leg opening (which is not our purpose here). For us, we shall try to make it an easier "Plough" pose, and a pose that does not restrict breathing as much. Once you have mastered it, you should gradually close the legs.

**b.**  Another way to ease in into the pose is to execute it **with one leg**; easier to perform and easier to breathe. When you become proficient, use it to ease into the final "two-legs" pose.

**c.**  You can also **use a prop** for the gradual stretching of the spine: Use a chair (eventually with a towel or a cushion) to support your feet above the ground. When you become proficient, gradually lower the height of support with other props until the feet reach the ground comfortably.

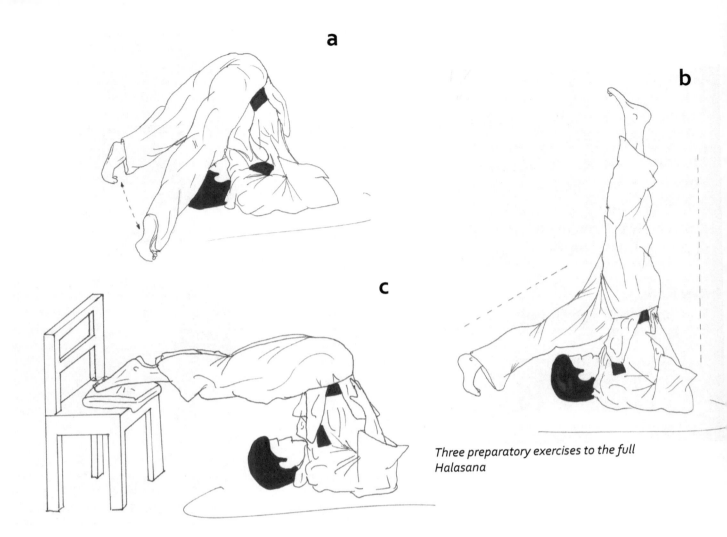

**a**

**b**

**c**

*Three preparatory exercises to the full Halasana*

This is an important drill and you should do everything possible to become able to hold the pose. Once you do and become more proficient, there are two variations of the pose that will stretch your spine even more:

- _Supta Paschimottasana_, or "Lying Down Westward Pose". From the Plough Pose, you lower your sit bones towards the floor and grab your feet to pull your knees towards your head. The legs are straight, and it is as if you fold yourself straight in two. This is stretching the lower back even more. Execute as per our agreed methodology.

- _Karnapidasana_, or "Pressure on the ears-Pose". From the Plough Pose, you bend your legs and lower the opened knees on the floor as close as possible to the ears. Catch the back of the knees with your arms and "round" yourself as much as possible. Proceed carefully, especially with the neck joint.

➤

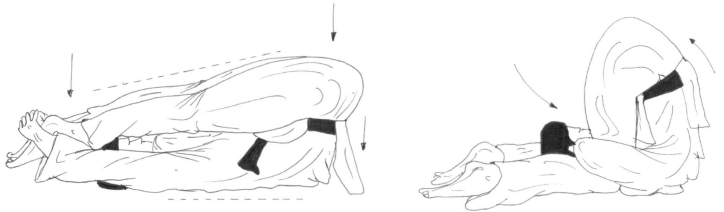

*The advanced poses, respectively Supta Paschimottasana and Karnapidasana*

*Different hands positions in Halasana*

*Supta Paschimottasana for extreme lower back stretch*

## 15.3 Sitting Side Bends

This is basically the same pose as the "Sitting Wide One-leg Side Stretch" presented in section 11.3.1 for adductors work. This time though, the emphasis is on the laterals and the legs need *not* be stretched open at their maximum. You should take the pose, *Yoga's Parivrtta Upavistha Konasana,* with your legs opened naturally at their un-stretched maximum. You then lean sideways and catch your toes as described in the coming Drawing. Concentrate on your sides and lower back, and refer to the Key Points of section 11.3.1.

*Concentrate on your Lateral Muscles*

The second Figure shows a preparatory exercise in which you lean sideways, with your fingers crossed behind your head, and place your elbow on the floor behind the extended knee.

*An easier pose to prepare Parivrtta Upavistha Konasana*

## 15.4 Standing Side Bends

This is a very simple stretch, to be drilled seriously and to its maximum each time according to our proper methodology. This is said because it is a pose easily looked down upon. From a standing position, lift your hands in prayer over your head and stretch upwards as much as possible to elongate your spine. Lean sideways gradually to your maximum. Then switch sides.

**Key Points:**

- *Stretch the spine* during the exercise.
- Keep the upper body *straight in line* (i.e. parallel to the wall in front of you); do not twist.
- *Concentrate* on your laterals and aim at reaching with your hands as far as possible.

*Lean Sideways while elongating the spine*

## 15.5  Seated Twist

This is the "Waist Twist" already presented in section 13.5 for glutei and hip belt work. But this time you will try to concentrate on (and emphasize) the lower back and laterals work, i.e. the twist *itself*.

The pose, presented again in the Figure is identical to the Waist Twist and the reader is therefore invited to refer to section 13.5.

*Eka Pada Parivrtta Upavisthasana, previously encountered*

As the twist is now the emphasis of the drill, there is a preparatory posture that works the laterals without being too difficult on the glutei, hip belt and leg muscles: *Yoga's Marichyasana III*. You simply execute the pose without placing the foot of your bent leg over the thigh of the straight leg. Bend the leg up and twist as much as you can; concentrate on the twist. Refer to the next Drawing and the coming Photo.

➡️

*Preparatory Pose to the Seated twist*

On the other hand, a more challenging pose would be *Ardha Matsyendrasana* (Half Lord of the Fishes Pose) in which you also bend the leg on which you are sitting.

*The more challenging Ardha Matsyendrasana*

*The easier Marichyasana III*

## 15.6  Extended Triangle

This is an iconic *Yoga* posture in which you will certainly feel your laterals stretching, especially at the beginning. You will also feel your hip belt and legs, as it is a very complete stretch, but try to concentrate on the waist. You start *Utthita Trikonasana*, the 'Extended Triangle Pose', from a wide open stance, one foot pointing forward and the other, on the same line, pointing obliquely 45 degrees. Lean sideways towards the front foot (pointing forward) and place the hand on the floor, near and behind the foot. Keep your body in line - *no twisting*-, and extend the other arm in-line towards the ceiling. Keep your legs straight. If you have difficulty to take the posture, place your down hand *on* the front leg, as low as possible, but at the height that allows you to take the pose and work on the side bend.

*Yoga's classic Utthita Trikonasana*

**Key Points:**

- Legs *straight*.
- No twisting; lean with *body in line.*
- Stretch *shoulders and spine.*


The pose can be executed with the hand on the floor *in front or behind* the leg, according to your progress.

*Utthita Trikonasana with hand in front or behind the extended leg. In all cases, look up at your hand*

# CHAPTER 16    UPPER BODY

*Of course, kicking involves the whole body. In order to have a complete work-out, and for general benefit, it is recommended to include some upper body flexibility training. A few exercises are suggested. I have often seen experienced Martial Artists in Yoga or Flexibility practice who were extremely flexible in their lower body, but who had extremely tight shoulders.*

*Upper Body Fitness is important to many kicks*

## 16.1  Pectoral Door-frame Stretch

This stretches the pectorals and the shoulders. It can be executed in a doorframe, hence the name, or on a wall corner. Refer to the Figure. Place the arm at shoulder height first, with the forearm bent at 90 degrees and therefore parallel to the door frame. Push your upper body forward to stretch your pectoral and anterior shoulder; you can also twist the body away if you keep the trunk straight. Treat this as a full stretch and use the right methodology to improve gradually. Switch arms. Once proficient you can start vary the arm height and the angling of the elbow for slightly different stretching effects.

*Pectoral doorframe Stretch; push the torso forward*

**Key Points:**
* Keep the *trunk straight*.
* Neck *erect* and look forward.

## 16.2 Pectoral Table Stretch

For this pectorals-and-shoulders-stretch, you can use a table or a dance bar or anything at the right height. It is a very common relaxing stretch; but treat it as a stretch to progress into. With straight legs and the body bent at 90 degrees, place your hands on the table and push your (straight) torso down. Concentrate on the stretch.

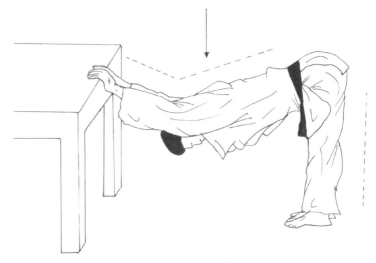

*Bend down to stretch the upper body*

### Key Points:
- Legs and arms *straight*.
- Trunk straight and *stays in line*.
- *Elongate spine*.

*Elongate spine while doing the Pectoral Table Stretch*

## 16.3 Elbow Back Pull

This is a very simple and beneficial shoulder stretch. Refer to the Illustration. With your arms behind your back, catch your elbow with the other hand and pull it in as much as possible. Try to gradually reach a bit more. Switch arms.

### Key Points:
- Keep your body *straight*; do not lean.
- Keep the stretched elbow *down and relaxed*.
- Pull the elbow sideways, *not up*.

*Pull the elbow in your back and stretch the shoulder*

## 16.4 Eagle Pose Grip

This is the typical hands position in the "Eagle" *Yoga* Pose, *Garudasana*. Like often in *Yoga*, the pose is more complex and stretches more muscles groups; in this case, the legs are also intertwined in a difficult fashion. For our purpose, we shall only drill the arm position illustrated in the Figures with close-up. It may seem simple, -cross your arms and place your palms together in prayer-, but many athletes with well-muscled shoulders will find it extremely difficult. Proceed gradually and strive for progress; this is a very important exercise for shoulder flexibility and resistance to injury.

*Eagle Pose Grip*

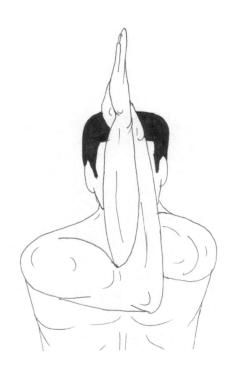 

*The hand position in Yoga's Garudasana*

### Key Points:

- Start by crossing your arms *as far as possible* at the elbows.
- Strive to place your palms *fully together* in prayer position; at the beginning, try to catch the thumb of the upper hands with the fingers of the lower hand.
- Start high; when proficient, *lower the locked hands* for further stretching.
- Keep upper body *straight*.

## 16.5   Back Namaste

The name of this stretch refers to the classic praying hands position of *Yoga*, the traditional "Namaste" greeting. But this time, you will have your hands take this position *in your back*. The idea, illustrated by the Figures and Photo, is simple; but the execution can be challenging. Proceed gradually and do not neglect this simple exercise that stretches the whole arm from the shoulder down.

*Back Namaste*

*Praying behind your back...*

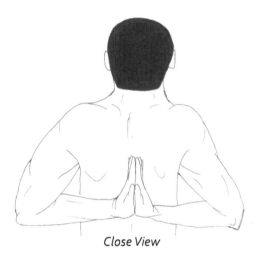

*Close View*

### Key Points:
- Keep body *straight*.
- Shoulders *low* and relaxed.
- Start by joining the fingers; then strive to get the palms together and as *high as possible*.

## If you can't outplay them, outwork them.
## ~Ben Hogan

## 16.6 Cow's Face Grip

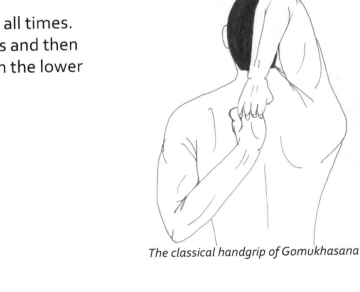

This, again, refers to a *Yoga* pose named "Cow Face", *Gomukhasana*. The pose is, again, more complex and involves a difficult cross-legged sitting posture. We shall only drill the particular hand grip of the pose. You can practice the stretch standing or sitting comfortably, as you like, as long as you make sure your back is straight. The posture is a well-known classic and is illustrated in the coming Drawings. Your hands grip one another in your back, with one arm from above and one from below. It is often very difficult, and often not symmetrically easy!

### Key Points:
- Body *straight* at all times.
- Grip your fingers and then *pull up* to stretch the lower arm.

*Cow's Face Grip*

*The classical handgrip of Gomukhasana*

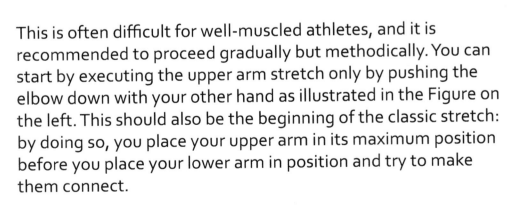

This is often difficult for well-muscled athletes, and it is recommended to proceed gradually but methodically. You can start by executing the upper arm stretch only by pushing the elbow down with your other hand as illustrated in the Figure on the left. This should also be the beginning of the classic stretch: by doing so, you place your upper arm in its maximum position before you place your lower arm in position and try to make them connect.

*Preparatory stretch to the Cow Face Grip*

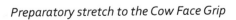

If you find it difficult to even connect, you should proceed with the help of a band or a towel. The Figure on the right shows, appropriately, the execution with a karate belt. You execute the drill with some distance between the hands but with the option to pull up. Strive to reduce gradually the distance between the hands until you can have your fingers grip one another. Maybe only two fingers at the beginning; then tighten gradually your grip with more fingers and finally a tighter grip. Pull!

*Use a belt to progress towards the full stretch*

*Grab with more and more fingers, then tighten gradually*

## 16.7   Downward Dog Pose

We have, of course already encountered *Yoga's* "Dog Poses" in section 9.2.1 for calves stretching. As mentioned, most *Yoga's* poses work on several different body areas at the same time. The "Downward Dog Pose", *Yoga's Adho Mukha Svanasana*, is also a great shoulder and spine stretch. Refer to section 9.2.2 and execute the pose while *emphasizing the shoulder stretch*. For this, you will need to execute the "long" dog, with more distance between your hand and feet, and push your chest and shoulders down as much as possible.

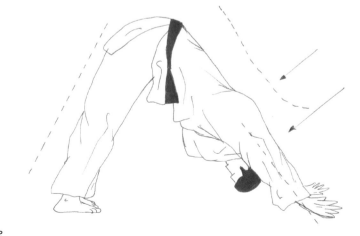

*Concentrate on the shoulder stretch in Downward Dog pose*

**Key Points:**

- Keep arms *straight*, legs *straight* and heels on the floor.
- *Concentrate* on the shoulders.
- *Lower the head and neck* as low as possible between your arms.

While in position, you could alternate the stretches: concentrating first on the posterior leg, and then on the shoulders.

## 16.8 Side Praying Grip

Again a simple but very effective shoulder stretch, that can also be executed any time, any place, as a relaxing exercise. As illustrated in the Photos, interlock your fingers behind your back as if in prayer; then bring the joined hands to one side. Strive to pull the hands *forward*. Switch sides.

**Key Points:**

- Elongate the spine and stay *straight*.
- Pull the joined hands *straight forward* to your front.
- Try to get *further* each time.

*Front and Back view of the Side Praying Grip; concentrate on pulling the "across" arm forward*

## 16.9 Wall Shoulder Stretch

This is a classic shoulder stretch. With your whole front arm against a wall and parallel to the ground, you twist your upper body as much as possible in the other direction. Switch sides.

➤

## Key Points:

- Make sure the whole arm and shoulder stay *in constant contact with the wall.*
- *Open palm,* on the wall.
- Twist the upper body and neck; *try to look over the other shoulder.*

*Arm and shoulder on the wall, stretch*

**Perseverance is the hard work you do after you get tired of doing the hard work you already did.**
**~Newt Gingrich**

# PART 3

# AFTERWORD AND OTHER DRILLS

Some readers would expect at this stage a list of training routines. As already mentioned, the author does not believe in setting fixed programs to be followed blindly. The reader should be an experienced Martial Artist and can easily build his own list of exercises in order of preference and follow it. Of course, all the previous advice should be heeded.

*In order to undergo the leapfrog to the next level*, the artist should pursue a methodical regimen of 4 to 5 weekly hours for at least three months, on top of his regular training. As mentioned, the preferred timetable should be: Plyo, Flex, Plyo, Flex, Plyo, followed by two rest days. One of the two rest days should also be a full rest day from _all_ other regular training.

The trainee is then invited to compile his training routine as per the drills he feels are most appropriate for his goals and physiology. For Plyometrics, the routine should include a mix of drills: both multi- and single response, both on-box and off-box types, and also drills involving kicking. For Flexiometrics, the routine should include stretches from all muscle categories described. *It is then of the highest importance that the trainee follow his weekly routine without changing it*. The exercises and their sequence should be fixed for at least one month but preferably three, in order to ensure maximum progress. (*As mentioned, the routines should be changed after three months, and comprise 50% new exercises from the book*). The trainee should then start drilling slowly, gradually and carefully, with rests in between exercises. The first Plyometrics sessions should comprise only 5 to 10 minutes of net plyometric work. The length of the plyo sessions, the difficulty and the speed can slowly be increased and the rest in between drills decreased. With training and increased familiarity, the trainee will finally do one full hour session of Plyos and Flexios with no rest in between drills and at his maximum performance level. It is not advised to train more than one hour for both types.

*All the while, the trainee will continue his regular training*: Martial Art classes in his chosen style and complementary training according to his goals. The Flexiometrics and Plyometrics presented here are only two types of complementary training for the athlete, the Martial Artist in general and the kicker in particular. There are many other training methods to improve one's performance; the author just feels that Plyometrics and Methodical Flexibility Training are the most beneficial and generally the most under-used. Other general categories of training methods are listed from here on, although the list is sketchy and certainly not exhaustive. Many drills are also cross-overs from different categories.

➤

### a. Rope Skipping

This is probably the most important of all, and it is rightly mentioned in this book: **Rope Skipping is in fact a classical PLYOMETRIC exercise!** It is multi-response and minimizes ground time. Rope skipping in its many forms, is probably the most effective exercise to develop the core muscles of the lower leg involved in fast movement and body positioning. Because we are constantly walking and standing, the calves and other muscles of our lower legs are very developed and extremely difficult to challenge. Heavy weight exercises are not what are needed to stimulate all the muscles involved in fast and all-directions moves. The best way, and probably the only way, is rope skipping for bouts of *at least* twenty minutes. It is time-consuming, unfortunately, but there is no way around it. For time-saving purposes, rope skipping was the author's favorite warming-up drill. Once one is familiar with regular skipping, it is recommended to up the challenge with more complex skipping and the gradual addition of weight by the way of ankle weights and/or a weight vest. Remember though, that weight is not at the heart of the drill: the key point is the multi-response stimuli to the calf muscles. Weight addition is only when the drill is completely mastered and executed fast and flawlessly.

### b. Kicking Drills

There are many kicking drills, well-known by the all Artists. Besides the very important technical work in one's chosen style, a few examples of classical drills are illustrated. *Not illustrated* here are the many possible combinations of Double Kicks, Triple Kicks and Feint Kicks.

*The classic "Squat and Kick*

*Another "Squat and Kick"*

*Kick/Chamber back/Pivot 90 degrees/Kick/Chamber back/ Pivot 90 degrees/etc etc...The foot does not go back to the floor*

*Spin-back down and kick up*

Crescent Kicks over a partner's hand

Chamber and kick over partner

Mark the floor and hop as far as possible while kicking

Another chambering over partner

Kick Focus pad for accuracy and right trajectory

Evade and Kick

**PLYO-FLEX**

*Kick from the ground*

Use of a dynamic stick for body positioning during kicking

*Stick training*

*Use of a static stick for body positioning during kicking*

*Use of a ladder for accurate kicking practice*

*Use of a belt for head height control during kicking*

*Use of a wall for correct trajectory work*

*Same-leg kicking in series, let the foot "rebound" on the floor. Execute at least 20 kicks before switching legs*

**PLYO-FLEX**

*Another kick and pivot 90 degrees with no ground touch. Keep at it*

*Repeated side kicking with no ground touch*

*Kick with hands tied up at guard level; Full kicking moves with hand movements neutralized for better balance and control*

*Kicking with hands tied behind back*

*Rebounding Front Kicks; using the floor as a springboard for kicks in series*

*Rebounding Roundhouse Kicks. Keep Kicking!*

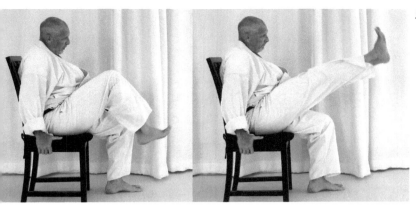

*Static Chair Kicking*

*Chair Kicking with hip push*

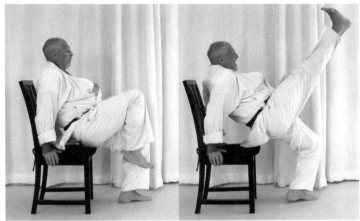

*Full Kick from chair-sitting*

Of course, this was a very limited illustrated list of examples. The number of possible kicking drills is immense.

## c. _Kicking Drills with Props_

The use of props for technical orthodoxy, target and trajectory practice has been hinted at in previous work. A few examples are presented here. Again, those are only a few of many.

_The use of targets like Body Shields and Focus Pads_

_The use of a chair for good chambering_

_The use of a chair and a focus pad or a heavy bag_

_The use of a chair and a boxing speedball_

_The use of a stick for spinning back drills_

192    **_PLYO-FLEX_**

The use of a medicine ball:
Spin-back ground hook kick and
downward heel "axe" Kick

The use of hanging
tennis balls for
accuracy- and "hooking"
effect-training

The use of a belt for
high chambering

The use of an old
tire for impact
and target
training

A heavy bag can
also be used on the
floor

The use of an elastic band between the knees. Many drills are possible

### d. Ankle Weights Kicks

Ankle weights or iron boots are an essential tool in kick-building. There is no better way to work the specific muscles involved in the kick than having to increase the effects of gravity. Always remember, after a series of weighted kicks, to immediately execute the kick a few times without weight. It is recommended, when working with ankle weights or iron boots (or ski boots), to pay particular attention to a technically perfect kick. For example, kicks requiring high chamber should be drilled with a chair or an obstacle ensuring this proper chamber. As mentioned, the author thinks that ankle weights combined with Plyometrics are for the extremely well-conditioned elite athletes only, because it requires well trained core muscles and joints (to prevent injury).

*Iron Boots- and Ankle Weights-kicking. Try to use props for good form and remember to always kick free-of-weight at the end of the drill*

### e. Isometrics and Dynamic Self-Resistance

**Isometrics** are a very safe and easy way to build the kicking muscles. They are by definition done in static positions. Theoretically, the joint angle and muscle length do not change during the muscle contraction. An example would be pushing to develop a kick against the wall ("overcoming isometrics": you cannot push the wall away) or maintaining the position against a partner's weight ("yielding isometrics": you could push the partner away if you wished to). Maintaining the leg in extended kicking position is another example of a truly isometric exercise, well-known in Martial Arts training halls. In fact, many *Yoga* balance exercises are extremely beneficial isometric exercises, as maintaining the position and balance requires the static work of many opposing muscle groups. Presented here, just as an illustration are the Chair Pose (*Utkatasana*) and the Warrior 3 Pose (*Virabhadrasana*).

*Isometric Training would be the best 'third tennet' of your regimen, as it is complementary to Plyo-Flex and the best way to build up basic strength. Our book 'The Isoplex Method' puts it all together with detailed training sessions that cobine Isometrics, Plyometrics and Flexiometrics.*

Front Kick Chamber against the sh-back of a partner, an example of yielding isometrics

*Examples of Yoga balance poses building muscle power isometrically: Respectively Utkatasana and Virabhadrasana*

*The airplane, a variation of the Virabhadrasana balance pose; isometric muscle-building exercise*

*Maintaining the leg in front kick position is also a great isometric exercise*

A close relative of Isometrics, is **Dynamic Self-Resistance**, in which you use your own muscles against their opposites. In this case, the muscle length does change, albeit very very slowly and against the resistance of another muscle group. This is the typical slow and hard forms (*Kata*) of the classical Okinawan styles of *Karate* like *Goju-ryu* or *Uechi-ryu*. An example would be the slow development of a kick with all muscles tensed, pitting quadriceps against hamstrings (among others).

After isometric and dynamic tension exercises, it is recommended to do a few fast and loose moves to relax the muscles involved.

# f.  *Weight Training*

Working the leg muscles is, of course, a basic requirement for the kicking artist. Squats and lunges should be drilled, but carefully on behalf of the knee joints. A muscle-building regimen should include work on all the leg's muscles: not only quads and hamstrings, but also abductors and adductors, and the glutei! And, of course, the laterals, abdominals and lower back are part of the kicking "lines of supply".

Muscles can be built with weight machines, free weights and weightless exercises. All types are valid and it is recommended, again, to stick to a specific exercise program for a minimum of one month and a maximum of three. Then, the program should change to new exercises and to new reps/sets combinations. Bodybuilding routines, methods and theories are beyond the scope of this book. A few photos will simply illustrate the subject.

*Abductors Machine*

*Adductor Machine*

*Leg Press Machine*

*Calf Machine*

*Leg Curl (Hamstrings) Machine*

*eg extension
(Quadriceps)
Machine*

*Gluteus work on
the rotary weight
machine*

## g.   *Balance Drills*

Balance drills are important in that they stimulate the entire set of little core muscles and ligaments involved in position correction. Those play a key role in fast movement and kick trajectory. Those exercises are often undeservedly neglected because they seem "easy" and "soft". Besides the "isometric" yoga poses already presented, the iconic "tree pose" is highly recommended, as it stimulates all the small core muscles of the lower leg that are difficult to exercise otherwise.

Another great drill is the standing, punching, kicking and "free sparring" atop "Bosu" balls (Bosu balance trainers) or related equipment.

*Yoga's Tree Pose, Virksasana*

## h.    Impact Training

There is no alternative to kick **into something** in order to learn to channel all power to the point of impact, in sports or in real combat. It is all the more important if the trainee has even the slightest fear of hurting his toes or other foot part when kicking, as it can unconsciously cause the body to slow the kick down. All kicks must be drilled for power development at impact and for the feeling of the force reaction, whether the power at impact comes from strength and hip thrust, or comes from speed. Heavy bags of all contents, forms and sizes, punching balls, focus pads, protected partners, tires, bean bags, Makiwara, ... everything goes. The *Shi-Heun* students regularly use end-of-season banana trees plantations for long sessions of impact training.

*Body shield and focus pad*

*Heavy bag hanging or on the ground*

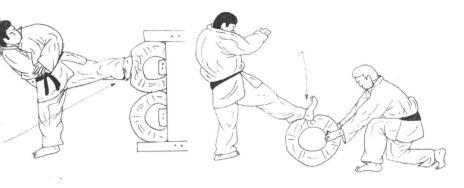 

*Old tire, fixed or hold by partner*

*The classic Japanese Makiwara*

*Standing bags of all types, with or without medicine ball on top*

*Boxing speed-ball or hanging tennis balls*

*...en the wall, padded or not, and old phonebooks*

# i.    _Angling, Trajectory Work and Ground Kicking_

In free or real fighting, your opponent will rarely stay in place and wait for your kicking. It is important to drill **angling** your kicks, **changing their trajectory** during delivery and delivering them **from unexpected positions**. Your Front Kick could go further with in-delivery hop. It could curve on delivery to sneak into your opponent's guard. It could be delivered while pivoting sideways to follow an evading adversary. A few examples are presented here, but there are many more.

1

_Two angling ways to drill the Roundhouse Kick_

2

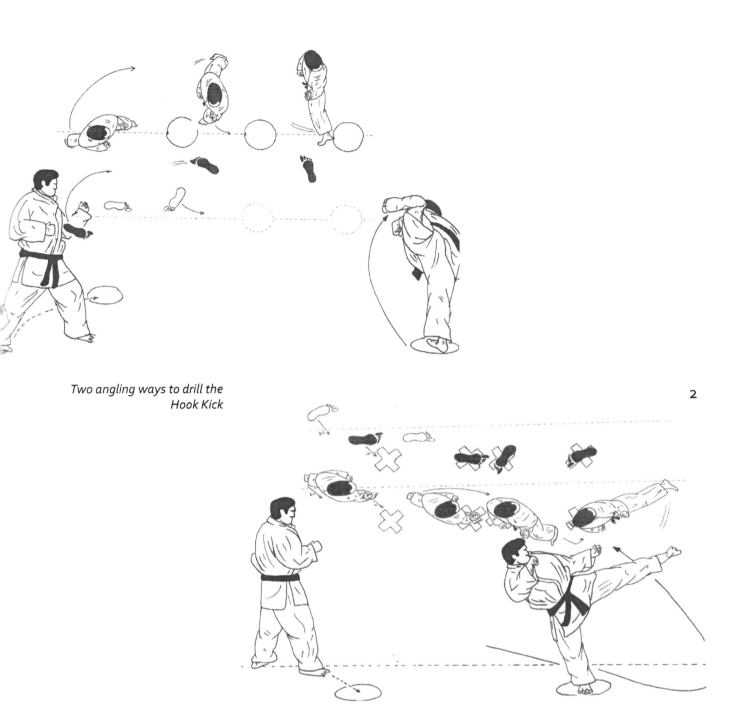

*Two angling ways to drill the Hook Kick*

2

**Ground Kicks** and **Dropping** (to the ground) **Kicks** are a great way to improve the corresponding "standing" Kicks. Not only does it teach you kicking from awkward or moving positions, it also makes you use all kinds of small muscles against gravity, muscles that do not encounter the same stress when kicking standing up. A few kicks are presented, as well as classical calisthenics/aerobic exercises relevant to this training angle.

*A ground version of the Front, Side and Back Kick; respectively*

*Ground Roundhouse Kick to the side; great for the hip muscles*

*Ground high back Kick*

*Side straight-leg lift; great muscle builder*

**PLYO-FLEX**

*Drop Ground Roundhouse Kick*

## j.   *Telegraphing*

Initiating kicks and combination attacks in front of the mirror or with a cooperating partner is an important drill. Look, or have him look at any telltales, shoulder drops, foot twitching, head bobbing, and others that would give away your imminent attack. You should strive to explode forward instantly, with no telegraphing. This is an exceedingly important kicking skill.

## k.   *Free-fighting*

There is no alternative to mix it all together in front of an opponent that moves, attacks, blocks, evades and counters. This should be preferably done with several sets of rules to familiarize the fighter with the fact that the rules of engagement always influence the way to fight. Besides light sparring and one's fighting in the framework of his school's rules, it is beneficial to learn to spar with different and also minimal rules for real-life closeness. Of course with caution and supervision.

*There is no alternative to Free-Fighting*

# COMPLEMENTARY READING

This Plyo-Flex book concentrates on the Plyometric ans Flexiometric Drills for the Martial Artist in general and the avid kicker in particular.

It presupposes that the Artist does also work on his strength development.

If the reader wants a more complete treatise on building athletic performance and a well-defined and effective musculature, we have presented a complete system in our book: "*The Isoplex Method*".

The preferred strength-building principle is definitely **Isometrics,** as shown by experience and touted by Masters like the late *Bruce Lee*. The book presents the Isometrics drills on top of the Plyometrics and Flexiometrics parts (that are beefed up with more exercises). On top of that "*The Isoplex Method*" presents fully detailed drilling programs, as it is written for the general public (and not focused on the Martial Artist).

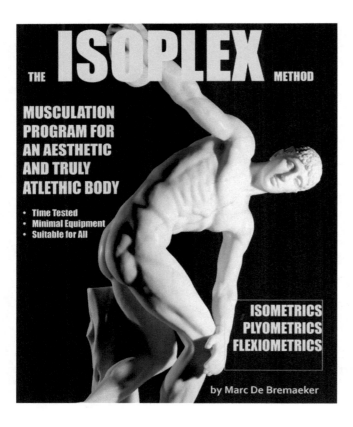

*Isoplex* stands for Isometrics, Plyometrics and Flexiometrics The well-organized combination of these three training methods will give the serious trainee the most effective path possible to powerful and aesthetic muscles, in a minimum of time. The method is simply the optimal combination of those three basic tenets of fitness training. It is suitable for men and women. It is suitable for beginners, for athletes of all types, and even for bodybuilders. It is designed to build an aesthetic physique which is also conducive to sport performance and to personal health.

ISOPLEX is in fact the modern and more scientific version of the training ideals of Greco-Roman Antiquity. As illustrated by many well-known antique sculptures, the athletes of old had aesthetic bodies based on core musculature and long, well-defined and necessarily efficient muscles. These synergistic training principles are and were universal. They were to be found in ancient Asian Martial Arts and in Body Cultures like Yoga, Chi Kung and many others. A truly athletic and functional body needed for realistic fighting was achieved by a mixture of Isometric exercises, intensive flexibility training and dynamic (Plyometric) drills. Martial Artists and Yogis will immediately grasp the connection. This is the way to train the body for effective and natural aesthetics, and that is what Isoplex concentrates on through an optimal and synergistic time-saving program.

With hundreds of Photos and Drawings and detailing Five complete weekly Programs for all levels.

I fear not the man who has practiced 10,000 kicks once, but I fear the man who has practiced one kick 10,000 times.
~ Bruce Lee

Pain is the best instructor, but no one wants to go to his class.
~Choi, Hong Hi, Founder of Taekwon-Do

Only one who devotes himself to a cause with his whole strength and soul can be a true master. For this reason mastery demands all of a person.
~Albert Einstein

*If you have enjoyed the book and appreciate the effort behind this series, you are invited to write a short and honest review on Amazon.com...It has become extremely difficult to promote one's work in this day and age, and your support would be much appreciated. Thanks!*

All questions, comments, additional techniques, special or vintage Photos about Kicks and Krav Maga are welcomed by the author and would be introduced with credit in future editions. Just email:**martialartkicks@gmail.com**

The author is trying to build a complete series of work that, once finished, could become an encyclopedic base of the whole of the Martial Arts-Kicking realm, a base on which others could build and add their own experiences.

In his endeavors the author has already penned:

- **The Essential Book of Martial Arts Kicks** – *Tuttle Publishing* (2010)
- **Plyo-Flex** - Training for Explosive Martial Arts Kicks (2013)
- **Low Kicks** - Advanced Martial Arts Kicks for Attacking the Lower Gates (2013)
- **Stop Kicks** – Jamming, Obstructing, Stopping, Impaling, Cutting and Preemptive Kicks (2014)
- **Ground Kicks** – Advanced Martial Arts Kicks for groundfighting (2015)
- **Stealth Kicks** - The Forgotten Art of Ghost Kicking (2015)
- **Sacrifice Kicks** - Advanced Martial Arts Kicks for Realistic Airborne Attacks (2016)
- **Krav Maga Kicks** - Real-world Self defense Techniques from Today's most effective Fighting System (2017)
- **Joint Kicks** - Destruction of the Opponent's Limbs (2018)

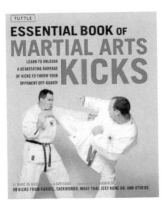   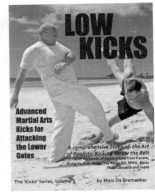

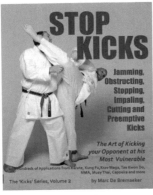 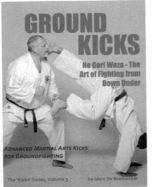 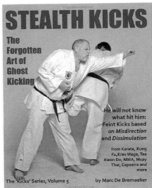 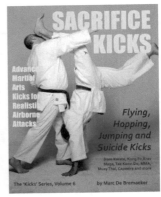

**Low Kicks** are powerful, fast, and effective exactly what you need to defend yourself in a real life confrontation. And because they are seldom used in sport fighting, they can be a surprising and valuable addition to your free fighting arsenal. While they may seem easy to execute, not all low kicks are simply low versions of the basic kicks. There are specific attributes and principles that make low kicks work. Marc de Bremaeker has collected the most effective low kicking techniques from Martial Arts like *Krav Maga, Karatedo, Capoeira, Wing-Chun Kung-Fu, MMA*, and *Muay Thai*. In this book, he analyzes each kick in depth, explaining the proper execution and outlining applications and variations from self-defense, sport fighting and traditional practice: Hundreds of examples in over one thousand photographs and drawings.

**Joint Kicks - Destruction of the Opponent's limbs.** Joint Kicks are probably the most effective way to neutralize an assailant in real-life situations. By attacking the opponent's articulations you ensure that they will not be able to keep on the fight; they will not be able to punch you with a damaged arm and they will not be able to run after you with a busted leg. Joint Kicks are basically regular kicks to be delivered towards specific targets and with the focused intention to cause damage. This is Martial arts in their purest sense and not sport techniques.

In real life, you could easily encounter an assailant with a high resistance to pain. It could the high adrenalin levels, alcohol intoxication or drugs. But will be very different from free-fighting in the dojo. If he is impervious to the pain of your blows, only **by** destroying the attacker's infrastructure will you be able to overcome him.

The book reflects on the mindset behind Joint Kicks and presents numerous examples of their use. With over 800 Photos and Drawings.

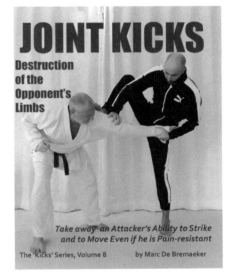

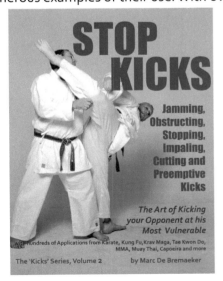

**Stop Kicks** are among the most effective, sophisticated kicks a fighter can use. And because they hit your opponent at his most vulnerable, they are also the safest way to pre-empt or counter an attack. Stop Kicks are delivered just as your opponent is fully committed to an attack, physically or mentally, meaning it is too late for him to change his mind. Hitting an opponent in mid-attack gives you the added advantage of using his attacking momentum against him. Stop Kicks: Jamming, Obstructing, Stopping, Impaling, Cutting and Preemptive Kicks presents a well organized array of stop-kicking techniques from a wide range of martial arts. Learn Pushing Kicks, Timing Kicks, Cutting Kicks, Obstruction Kicks, and Block Kicks from the hard-hitting styles of Muay Thai, Karatedo, Krav Maga, Tae Kwon Do, MMA and more.

Whether you are on the ground by choice or you have been taken down, whether your opponent is standing or is on the ground with you, whether you are a good grappler or you are trying to keep a good grappler at bay, whether you were caught unawares sitting on the floor or you have evaded down on purpose, whether you are a beginner or an experienced martial artist...this book has the right kick for the situation. In **Ground Kicks**: Advanced Martial Arts Kicks for Ground-fighting from Karate, Krav Maga, MMA, Capoeira, Kung Fu and more, Marc De Bremaeker has created a comprehensive collection of Ground Kicks, with hundreds of applications for sport fighting and self-defense situation. Packed with over 1200 photographs and illustrations, Ground Kicks also includes specific training tips for practicing each kick effectively.

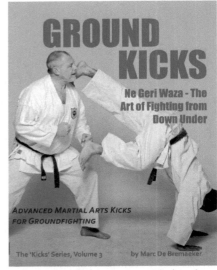

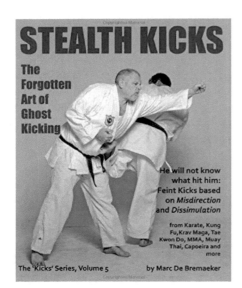

**Stealth Kicks** will introduce you to the Art of executing Kicks that your opponent will not see coming. This subject has never been treated comprehensively before. Whether you are a beginner or an experienced Artist, you will find suitable Kicks or tips to modify your current techniques to give them stealth. It will help you to score in Sport confrontations or make sure to come on top in real life Self-Defense situations. The *Feint Kicks* presented are based on misdirection: they will aim at provoking a misguided reaction that will open your adversary to the real kick intended. The *Ghost Kicks* presented are based on dissimulation and will travel out of your opponent's range of vision to catch him unawares. Together with general feinting techniques and specific training tips, hundreds of applications will introduce you to the sneaky Art of stealth kicking and will make you a better and unpredictable fighter. Crammed with over 2300 photos and drawings for an easy understanding of the concept of Stealth.

**'Sacrifice Kicks'** will comprehensively present the most important Martial Arts Airborne Kicks: Flying Kicks, Hopping Kicks, Jumping Kicks and Suicide Kicks. They have been dubbed 'Sacrifice' in the spirit of Judo's redoubtable Sutemi Takedowns in which one sacrifices his balance in order to throw his opponent down. *Flying Kicks* are not about showmanship, they are very effective techniques when used judiciously. They need not be necessarily high and spectacular; they can be surprising *Jumping Kicks* and *Hopping Kicks* executed long and low. And *Suicide Kicks* take the Sacrifice principles a little further: they are extremely unexpected techniques delivered airborne, but with little hope of landing on one's feet, unlike classic Flying Kicks. All these realistic maneuvers, coming from Karate, Krav Maga, Kung Fu, TaeKwonDo, MMA, Capoeira, Muay Thai and more, are described with applications and training tips. Over 1000 Photos and Illustrations.

# KRAV MAGA KICKS

**Tested in battle:**

**Kicking for No-nonsense Self-preservation**

*Real-world Self Defense techniques from today's most effective Fighting System*

The 'Kicks' Series, Volume 7       by Marc De Bremaeker

*Krav Maga* is recognized as one of the most efficient fighting systems around today. Based on common sense, it has evolved by necessity in a region ravaged by fighting for over a century. The first part of this book details and illustrates the preferred Kicks used in Krav Maga, and the second part presents the vital points to be targeted when kicking or striking. The Last part of this work is basically a full Krav Maga Self-defense course that also includes offensive techniques. The defenses against strikes, kicks, grabs, holds and chokes do often include kicking, but only when it is the most adequate reaction. This book is the first to underline in print the important principle of *Retzev*, with dozens of examples of continuous motion until the opponent is fully vanquished. Suitable for beginners and trained Martial artists from other Schools. **Over 1500 Photos and Illustrations!**

**ADVANCED KRAV MAGA**

**A Complete Reference**

Tested in Battle: Real-world Self-Defense techniques from today's most effective Fighting System

by Marc De Bremaeker, *author of 'Krav Maga Kicks'*

*NEW !*

*ADVANCED KRAV MAGA: A Complete Reference.*

Krav Maga is recognized as one of the most efficient fighting systems around today. Based on common sense, it has evolved by necessity in a region ravaged by fighting for over a century. This book completes the previous 'Krav Maga Kicks' by the same author, with the more advanced Krav Maga techniques. This encyclopedic work recapitulates Krav Maga's history and principles and covers again the opponent's vulnerable points to be targeted. It then goes on to describe the Strikes, Kicks and Special Techniques used commonly in KM. After covering the Theory of Aggression, it does detail advanced Offensive Techniques including Range Covering, Guard Neutralization and Naturally-flowing Combinations. The main body of the text will then cover Defenses against an opponent armed with a stick, a knife or a gun. The last part describes the use of everyday objects as Improvised Weapons.

All along, the book underlines continuously the cardinal Krav Maga principle of *Retzev*, with dozens of examples of 'continuous offensive motion' until the opponent is fully vanquished.
The 250 printed pages, suitable for beginners and trained Martial Artists from other Schools, are crammed to the brim with over 1500 Photos and Illustrations!

# OTHER GENRES FROM FONS SAPIENTIAE

AVAILABLE IN PAPERBACK AND KINDLE FORMATS ON AMAZON

**The Manual** is the definitive guide to Enhanced Concentration, Super Memory, Speed Reading, Note-Taking, Rapid Mental Arithmetic, and the *Ultimate Study Method* (USM).

The techniques presented are the culmination of decades of practical experience combined with the latest scientific research and time-tested practices. The system described herewith will allow the practitioner to:

• Read faster with higher comprehension.
• Remember any type of information instantly.
• Store information in long-term memory.
• Enhance concentration and focus.
• Access deeper levels of the mind.
• Induce relaxation.
• Rapidly perform complex mental arithmetic.
• Master the Ultimate Study Method (USM).

**USM** is a synergistic combination of established techniques for Concentration, Long-Term Memory, Speed Reading, and Note-Taking. It involves a systematic procedure that allows the practitioner to study any topic fast, efficiently and effectively. USM can be applied to all areas of educational study, academic research, business endeavours, as well as professional life in general.

<u>**Rain Fund**</u>: A riveting thriller

"...For the safety of the readers, this book ought to come with the disclaimer: leave this book read half-way at your own risk. Unless you are Superman, you won't be able to concentrate on much else until you have read the last page of "Rain Fund". The time has come for Patterson, Ludlum, Dan Brown et al to slide over and make space at the top for Marc Brem." - Shweta Shankar for Readers' Favorite

"...In the good tradition of Ludlum and Grisham. Five Stars" Aldo Levy

"Autistic geniuses charting financial markets; Mobster-fuelled Ponzi schemes; sophisticated hardware viruses; spies; and a rising superpower that strives for dominance – so realistic it is frightening."

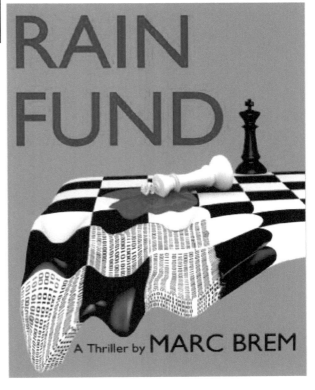

**PLYO-FLEX**

Printed in Poland
by Amazon Fulfillment
Poland Sp. z o.o., Wrocław

10065648R10121